JUSTICE IN MODERN ISLAMIC POLITICS

BY
Moustafa Elshami

Content

1. **INTRODUCTION**   01-24
   - 1.1 Semitic Religions
   - 1.2 Indian Religions
   - 1.3 East Asian Traditions
   - 1.4 Greeks

2. **QUR'ĀNIC CONCEPT OF JUSTICE**   25-94
   - 2.1 Definition of Justice in Islam
   - 2.2 The Qur'an on Justice
   - 2.3 Distributive Justice in Islam
   - 2.4 Political Justice in Islam
   - 2.5 Human Rights in Islam
   - 2.6 Women's Status in Islam
   - 2.7 Slavery in Islam
   - 2.8 Concept of Labour in Islam

3. **REVIEW OF THE CONCEPT OF JUSTICE IN CLASSICAL MUSLIM PHILOSOPHY**   95-123
   - 3.1 The Khawarij
   - 3.2 The Murjia
   - 3.3 The Jabriyah
   - 3.4 The Qadariyah
   - 3.5 The Mutazilah
   - 3.6 The Ashairah
   - 3.7 The Shī'ah

4. CONCEPT OF JUSTICE IN MODERN MUSLIM THOUGHT 124-152
    4.1   Shah Wali Allah (1703-1762)
    4.2   Jamal al-Din al-Afghani (1898-1897)
    4.3   Abul Ala Maududi (1903-1979)
    4.4   Sayyed Qutb (1906-1966)
    4.5   Murtada Mutahhari (1919-1979)
    4.6   Ali Shariati (1933-1977)

5. CONCLUSION   153-161

CHAPTER - I

INTRODUCTION

Justice is one of the four cardinal values and virtues. It is treated as one of the primary values and Ethico-Socio-Political-Legal and religious concepts. It is a highly fascinating and bewildering concept and has been variously discussed by the philosophers. Legal experts and socio-religious thinkers and interpreters of the religious texts have been playing a very crucial and critical role in the civilizational development of man. In the present work, various dimensions of the meanings and applications of justice have been discussed.

Man is profoundly and inextricably rooted in history. His history itself is rooted in pre-history. It will take large-scale investigations to somewhat bring out our rootedness in history and pre-history. Whatever empirical historical investigations have been available to us, reveal that human history is red in tooth and claw. Historical investigations inform us about insurmountable and excruciating amounts of suffering negotiated by human beings. They have negotiated incalculable oppression, suppression, exploitation and injustice. Countless people have been enslaved across history and globe.

Human beings have undergone a long-drown-out biological and cultural evolution. There are many theories with regard to the origin and development of man. All these theoretical perspectives advance their justificatory grounds which have been analyzed and criticized on genuine grounds by various thinkers. These theoretical perspectives are neither empirically verifiable nor mathematically demonstrable. They are not statements of fact but interpretative formulations. We can only appreciate the merits and demerits of these large-scale theological, cosmological and anthropological perspectives. However, scientists, paleontologists, anthropologists and historians have assembled vast data, powerfully indicating that man has negotiated millions of years of biological and cultural evolution. We do not have any definite accounts of the times and climes of man's post-evolutionary phase. However, what can be readily admitted is that his post-evolutionary phase of the struggle for existence must have been as indomitable as his pre-evolutionary biological evolution. The ancient human beings survived on wild fruits, leaves, vegetables, hunting, and fishing. This must have been a phase of unlimited competition over naturally grown eatables. After several million years, man could discover or explore agricultural process of production and cultivation. The agricultural mode of cultivation inaugurated a new phase in human history. It led to intense competition for agricultural lands and cultivation of numerous crops. Those who had the muscle power appropriated large agricultural fields for cultivation and employed landless labourers with a view to cultivating their crops. Thus, slowly and steadily, started the story of masters and slaves on a global scale. The agricultural fields led to clusters of inhabitants around them. These clusters became villages which graduated to towns and towns expanded into cities. Thus, we have millions of villages, thousands of towns and hundreds of large cities across and around the globe. The evolutionary process ultimately led to the emergence of major civilizations such as Babylonian civilization, Egyptian civilization, Chinese civilization, Indian civilization, Roman civilization etc. This phase of human evolution is marked by great rivalries, great competition, great struggles for domination, coercion and exploitation.

Small-scale villages turned into city-states and city-states, in course of time, expanded into vast kingdoms and empires. These large empires resulting in vast social, political and economic interactions led to great philosophical introspections, axiological debates, ideological recommendations, metaphysical perspectives, theological meta-narratives and great religions and value-systems came into being.

1.1 SEMITIC RELIGIONS

Thousands Semitic Prophets taught mankind the ethical virtues of peace and justice necessarily emanating from monotheistic commitments. Judaism, Christianity and Islām are the three great living manifestations of the Semitic religious tradition.

The Semitic religions advance a radically monotheistic world-view and value-system. They hold that the entire universe is a creature of the Supremely Powerful Creator, call Him God, Jehovah, or Allah. He is the Originator, Evolver, Cherisher, and Shaper of the universe. This universe is a purposeful creation of God. This vast universe is not a purposeless, directionless and meaningless adventure. The universe as a multi-complex space-time continuum is not readily transparent to human powers of understanding. The mystery of the cosmos is understood by the Creator of the universe. However, man has been given guidance by God through the agency of

Prophethood. In fact, the first created man Adam was himself a Prophet of God. Thereafter, thousands of Prophets were sent to thousands of settlements with a view to preach the monotheistic beliefs and values to human beings at different stages of history. These Prophets from Adam to Muhammad preached theocentricity of the highest order. The Messengers of God underlined that God should be the cynosure of all human actions and interactions. For God is the First and the Last, the Manifests and Hidden. We have come from God and we have to return to God. He is our Origin and He is our Destiny. The entire universe in its phenomenal complexity, is a system of signs indicative of the reality of God. Human beings have to conduct themselves through the understanding of the scriptural revelations and guidelines. God has bestowed upon all human beings certain capabilities, talents as well as powers of understanding and execution. Corresponding to their capabilities, talents and powers, they can be assigned various social, political, economic, intellectual and cultural projects or missions. These assignments entail offices and institutions of authority, promulgation and execution, administration and implementation. Accordingly, these offices of authority and decision also entail certain duties and responsibilities. The greatest duty and responsibility of any man is to respect the human rights of all and deliver or administer justice. Man must respect human rights and deliver justice, for, according to the Semitic creed, he will be resurrected on the Day of Judgment to give an account of his conduct during his sojourn upon the earth. The righteous people will be rewarded with the blessings of paradise and the vicious one would be consigned to hellfire.

JUDAISM

The Jews hold that justice is established when human beings operate in keeping with the commandments of God. In order to establish justice, human beings have to imitate God's attribute of justice. The Old Testament lays emphasis on the value of each human being. We are commanded, "you shall love neighbour as yourself, and you shall love the stranger as yourself" (Kessler, E. 2000, p. 72).Such commandments are central to the Jewish understanding of justice. They bring out the Jewish emphasis on the significance of every human person. In view of the same, Judaism underlines the importance of justice for every person. The slaves are to be treated with dignity. The orphans and widows are to be looked after. The strangers are to be taken care of. Even the prisoners of war cannot be divested of their human rights. The emphasis on the significance of every human being indicates that all people are finally of equal importance and should be treated with equal dignity. All human beings have one divine parent. Each individual is a potential progenitor of an entire new world. "Each one of us is entitled to see ourselves as the reason for the creation of the human race. Each individual is a unique creation" (Ibid, P. 73).

The Old Testament holds that each human being has a special status and is regarded as a child of God. Each human being is as if divinely sealed. Every human has certain fundamental rights which cannot be taken away from him. The Bible teaches that we are fundamentally human beings, not subjects and rulers, not slaves and masters etc. Each one of us is a person. Our neighbours exist in their own rights in God's image. Just as we are a people so they too are a people. Secondly moral law is above all laws. All human beings including the so-called kings, rulers, masters, subjects and slaves are bound by the moral law. All men have to respond to the imperatives of the moral law. The moral Law entails that man translate its imperatives into action. It is wrong to endanger the life and property of a human being. Man has to control all evil tendencies. He should to be kind and loving to his fellow human beings. Judaism teaches that a man should be especially responsible towards the weaker sections of the society, such as the orphans, the widows, the elderly people, the handicapped and the poor. These disadvantaged sections of the society have to be accorded equal respect for each human being bears the 'divine seal'. An ideal Jewish global society is a society of justice; all human beings are like a family and have to respect each other as brothers and sisters. In its understanding of justice, Judaism underscores the dignity and value of each human being. It stresses on the equality of all human beings and it emphasises one's responsibility towards disadvantaged sections of humanity.

CHRISTIANITY

In the Sermon on the Mount, Jesus brings out that his mission was not to destroy the law of prophets but to fulfil it. As an ethical teacher Jesus was more a reformer of the Hebrew tradition and a radical innovator. Jesus did not discard the old Hebrew teachings, he did not try to develop a comprehensive ethical system. Christianity retained the Jewish conception of morality as a divine Law appropriated to the interpretation of the word of God revealed through Scriptures.

Historically speaking, when Christian struggled its way to social and political power in the vast Roman Empire, its distinctively Hebrew or Semitic Theo-centric morality did change the moral climate of Europe and other parts of Empire. From the perspective of justice, the most vital change was a new sense of the equality of all human beings. Christians underlined that all human beings are equal because of their potential immortality. More importantly, they are equal because they are equally honourable in the eyes of God. Christianity is a religion of love and peace. In its struggle to establish peace, love and justice, it affected the larger part of western world.

Despite the heavy ethical orientation of Christianity, there was no systematic Christian ethical philosophy till Saint Augustine (354-430) who fashioned a distinctively Christian Ethics.

SAINT AUGUSTINE

Augustine (354-430) was one of the greatest Christian philosophical theologians. He negotiated numerous currents of thought such as Manichaeism, Skepticism, Platonism, Stoicism etc, before he finally graduated to Christianity. Most importantly, Augustine was impacted by Plato's social and political philosophy. However, Plato's social and political philosophy is given a Christian turn by Augustine. For Augustine, justice and peace are the cardinal virtues of the City of God.

According to Augustine, "justice is that virtue which gives to each his own" (Dunning, 1966, p. 158). As a Christian theologian, Augustine finds his conception of God intimately linked to justice. As a community we cannot meet out the imperatives of justice if we are not oriented to God. Without faith in God, we cannot but give ourselves to demons. By alienating ourselves from God we deny to God what is due to Him. Justice cannot be sustained in a community which is alienated from or disoriented to God. Augustine underlines that only justice can ethically hold a society together and where there is no justice, there cannot be peace. Justice signifies another name of the right relation of man and God. Where there is no justice, there cannot be any law. It is justice that distinguishes a state from the band of brigands (Ibid).

For Augustine, justice is something innate to the order of human beings. Man is innately oriented to a certain just order of nature. It is through this order of nature by which the soul is subordinated to God and the body is subordinated to the soul. In this way both soul and body are subordinated to God. Man's love of God is the springwell from which justice flows. Justice flows from the love of God as manifested in the love of others. However, despite man's innate spiritual orientation to God or love of God, he does reside in the city of man and therefore, for all practical purposes, man is centred on the love of self rather than on the love of God. In view of the same, the city of man is effectively devoid of charity and love. Accordingly, the city of man is devoid of true justice. The following words of Augustine are apt in this regard:

> So when man lives by the standard of truth he lives not by his own standard, but by God's. For it is God who has said, 'I am the truth.' By contrast, when he lives by his own standard, that is by man's and not by God's standard, then inevitably he lives by the standard of falsehood...Falsehood consists in not living the way for which he was created . . . And hence the falsehood: we commit sin to promote our welfare, and it results instead in our misfortune; or we sin to increase our welfare, and the result is rather to increase our misfortune (Krause, 2018, pp. 1-2). (https://www.printfriendly.com/p/g/t6PFAZ).

According to Augustine, if human beings are not guided by the light of truth, they get entangled in the lust for domination and ethos of coercion. For the proper dispensations of justice, human being needs to be appropriately subordinated to God. The fallen human beings, on their own, cannot dispense justice. True justice belongs to the order of God or the order of truth.

The city of man, according to Augustine, is wholly devoid of justice. Augustine says that justice in the city of man is deeply flawed. Social justice is negotiated through the realization of common good anchored on love of God in man. It's not the case that there is no justice in the city of man. However, the justice delivered in the city of man is incomparable to the justice dispensed with by recourse to love of God and love of the creatures of God.

According to Augustine, with reference to justice, man is on the horns of a dilemma. He is caught in between the love of self and the love of God. He is driven by the love of self and thwarted by love of God. He is guilty of wrongdoing or injustice and also coercion of being a wrongdoer or unjust. The Fall of Man or the Original Sin has corrupted him. However, it has not completely wiped out his conscience or soul. It is true that in the city of man, human beings are primarily driven by retributive justice, which more often than not, prevents reconciliatory justice from happening. The Fall of Man has oriented man towards coercion, domination and exploitation; however, human beings still retain some signs of their original condition such as justice.

Justice, according to Augustine, signifies conformity to order and respect for duties emanating from that order. Like Plato, Augustine believes that an individual is just if he fulfils those duties. However, there is a vital difference between Plato and Augustine. In case of Plato an individual's duties stemmed from the authority of the state and his duties were deemed to conform to the order of the state. In case of Augustine, an individual's duties were essentially religious and they should conform to the order of the Church which directs man towards God. For Augustine, justice, like Plato is not bound by space and time. Augustine does not deem the state to be the final society. Apart from the state there is a universal order of justice which according to Augustine is the Christian Commonwealth.

In his City of God, Augustine defends the meaning and significance of Christian beliefs and values. He rejects the contention of those who argued that Christians by undermining traditional Roman values, precipitated the fall of Roman Empire. Rather, Christianity advanced support to just rulers and legitimate governments. It promoted the welfare of the society by its faith in the God of history and by its moral teachings. Justice in the City of Earth can be achieved best by acknowledging the transcendent reality of the City of God.

God is Omnipotent and good and yet we cannot help admitting moral evil and explaining it as satisfactorily as possible. The supreme end of moral life i.e. happiness, can be found only in God. God has revealed His way by recourse to Jesus Christ. He has established Church with a view to establish God's Kingdom on earth. However, man is capable of doing any evil and his nature is utterly corrupt. There is no possibility of man saving himself but by recourse to the grace of God. Every man participates in the original sin of Adam and the fallen man can be saved by the grace of God only. Man on his part as a participant in the original sin cannot do any good or justice. Only God's grace can overcome man's propensity to doing evil.

According to Augustine, justice is one of the cornerstones of all political societies. Justice is the foundation of any State. Devoid of justice, any kingdom is nothing but a gang of criminals on a large scale. No republic can exist without justice. Justice is the most important function of the State. It is true that only God can deliver supreme good and supreme justice. Even then, the nobility of any political State depends upon justice.

Augustine's view of the State does not prevent him from realising the importance of the State in human society. The Fallen Man has acquired coercive and domineering attitudes. Therefore, Augustine does not trust the state to be capable of delivering complete justice. The State cannot socially engineer such human beings who are oriented to the city of God where absolute justice is delivered. However, the very concept of justice implicitly acknowledges sympathy and empathy for others. Justice without the cognizance of others is impossible of meaning. Justice is social and relational by its very nature. Justice implies a social and political sphere of action and operation. Justice as the highest virtue is rooted in the faith. In view of the same, all Christians should be deeply concerned about the delivery or dispensation of justice. It is by living with justice that one lives in accord with God. A true Christian will never violate the property or body of any other person, for his own satisfaction and domination. A true Christian is one whose lust for domination is controlled to the extent humanly possible. Human beings have traces of their original condition intact and they can return to goodness or justice not by their moral struggle but by the grace of God. However, the struggle for justice should be ceaseless in view of the fact that we are perennially oriented to coercion and domination. Human struggle for justice will always remain imperfect. Nevertheless, man is to continue to struggle for justice by recourse to love of God and man.

1.2 INDIAN RELIGIONS

Hinduism

India has been the mother of various cultures and civilizations. It has fostered various value-systems and ways of life. While modern western philosophers have formulated radical philosophical critiques of religion, the Indian seers have understood their beliefs and values by recourse to intuition and religious experience. Indian religious thought is anchored on intuition and religious experience. Indian seers and spiritualists have claimed that their profound religious and philosophical insights have been vouchsafed to them through the abiding supernatural and spiritual sources of both natural phenomena and human agents. The universe we are living within is divinely directed and God has divulged to seers and spiritualists the verities with regard to the alpha and omega of the universe. These seers and spiritualists have also been intimated the norms of righteous life paving the way for human liberation.

Hinduism as a way of life and as a philosophy of life cannot be neatly defined or summarized. It is characterized by numerous rather divergent strands of thought. Numerous textual resources justify divergent interpretations of Hindu beliefs and values. There are theistic and absolutistic, monotheistic and pantheistic, non-dualistic and dualistic strands of thought embodied in the metanarrative characterized as Hinduism. Accordingly, numerous philosophical perspectives have been put on Hindu religion and thought. The mainstream Hindu philosophy as derived from Vedas, Upanishads and Gita postulate a kind of unity of being in which the Supreme Reality or Brahman is equated with human soul or Atman and the world is also deemed to be only apparently real. The mystical union of human soul with the Supreme Reality is deemed to be the highest goal of life. At this level human spirit achieves its highest possible elevation. Such a spiritual experience intimates to us the ineffable joy and peace. Such a union with Supreme Reality constitutes the ultimate culmination of our spiritual struggle and religious commitment. It is the highest stage of human awareness, illumination and enlightenment. It is through such spiritual experience that we overcome our alienation from God. Shankaracharya, an advocate of unqualified non-dualism, underlines that such an experience is the realization of the identity of individual soul with the Brahman. Such a realization is an unavoidable condition for our liberation. Merger with Brahman is the final goal of the soul.

Human soul is caught into the eternal and inexorable law of karma. The past, the present, and the future; the social, political, economic, cultural and spiritual status of man has always been determined by our good or bad actions. Hinduism through its various textual resources asks human beings to abide by the imperatives of righteous or *dharma*. Human beings have to carry out their duties both as ordinary persons and as persons belonging to various castes such as Brahmins, Kshatriyas, Vaishyas and Shudras; the teaching class, the ruling class, the earning class, and the serving class respectively. Human beings are born into these higher and lower castes because of the actions they have accumulated in their previous birth or births. Apart from general duties such as being honest, being truthful, being kind, being helpful etc, they have to carry out their caste duties as well. It is the duty of Brahmins to learn scriptures, teach scriptures and conduct various types of religion ceremonies. The Kshatriyas have to be courageous, undergo military training and rule the country by defending it both from external aggression and internal rebellion. The Vaishyas have to carry out agricultural, industrial and commercial operations with a view to sustaining the economy of the country. The Shudras have to be labourers, workers or servants and help other castes in carrying out their numerous operations. The promotion in the next birth or liberation from the cycle of birth and rebirth depends upon the performance of caste duties in the sojourn of this birth upon the planet. Thus, according to Hinduism the social, political, and economic status of a human being is predetermined by his previous births. We can achieve social, political and economic rights or justice if we elevate ourselves morally and spiritually here and now during this very birth. *Bhagavad-Gita* brings out that man can achieve liberation either through path of devotion *(Bhakti Marg)*, path of action *(Karma Marg)* and path of knowledge *(JnanaMarg)*. The Yogis carry out profound concentrations and contemplations with view to understanding the very core of being. They try to break free of such beliefs, categories or constructions as are imposed upon us by our cultural conditioning. Thus, they try to achieve *Smadhi* which liberates them from dilemmas and paradoxes of Being. They try to achieve trans-consciousness of the primordiality of Being leading to transcendental peace and bliss (Sharma, 1987, pp. 15-16).

JAINISM

One of the oldest religions of India is Jainism. History of Jainas can be traced to the times immemorial. The Jainas believe in the teachings of twenty-four *Tirthankaras*, the first *Tirthankara* being Rishabhadeva and the last one being Vardhaman more popularly known as Mahivira of sixth century B.C. The Jainas are not oriented to faith in God. They follow the teachings of *Tirthankaras*, who had liberated themselves from bondage by recourse to excruciating moral and spiritual struggle and achieved perfection, omniscience, omnipotence and bliss. Following in the footsteps of *Tirthankaras*, Jainas hold that every human being has the capacity to attain to perfect knowledge, power and joy.

Jainas have formulated a detailed epistemological and metaphysical philosophy. Such Jaina doctrines as *Syadavada* and *Anekantavada* have led to a very powerful liberal, pluralistic and catholic orientation of Jaina philosophy. Jainas, like most other schools of Indian philosophy, accept attainment of liberation as the ultimate end of life. In order to achieve liberation, Jainas have formulated a strict ethical code of conduct. Accordingly, they have recommended five great vows:

Firstly, it is the duty of Jainas to practise *ahimsa* or non-violent. They have to be absolutely non-violent towards human beings, animals, living bodies in water, insects and plants upon the earth. Life is respectable wheresoever it is. No authentic Jainas can ever think of taking any life or encouraging others to take any life. Respect towards all life is unqualified and absolute.

Secondly, Jainas are exhorted to always tell the truth. We should speak truth under all conditions and speak in a good and blessed manner. The cultivation of truthfulness entails that a Jaina must also control anger, fear and greed.

Thirdly, it is obligatory on every Jaina to abstain from stealing. The property of anyone is as sacred as anyone's life. Non-violence and non-stealing, are integral to each other. In case we steal someone's property, we are ipso facto depriving him of the very condition of life.

Fourthly, the Jainas are exhorted to practise *Brahnacarya*. The ascetic must practise absolute celibacy. The masses are asked to be chaste. A true Jain must always abstain from self-indulgence. He must restrain himself from all forms of pleasure. He must control his thoughts, speech and deeds.

Fifthly, the Jainas are asked to practise *Aparigraha*. The ascetics should not own any property. The masses are asked to reduce their wants to the minimum possible. A true Jaina abstains from all attachments to the objects of the world. He is not addicted to pleasant sounds, touches, colours, tastes and smells. It is through detachment that liberation can be attained.

A Jaina who follows these five vows becomes capable of attaining perfect knowledge, perfect faith and perfect conduct. It is through such knowledge, faith and conducts that we can overcome the bondage of passions and *karmas* and attain to liberation (Mahadevan, 1974, pp. 102-103).

Thus, Jainas teaches that we can achieve a perfect social, political and economic order if we can become non-violent, have courage to speak the truth, do not eat up anyone's properties, abstain from self-indulgence and cultivate detachment from world. It can be readily admitted that wide-spread violence across history has been one of the main sources of injustice. In fact, human history has been a long-drawn-out unfoldment of political violence, economic exploitation and social injustice. If we can cultivate ethic of non-violence, we can to a large extent, succeed in controlling injustice and ushering in a just social order. Similarly, an ethic of non-stealing and detachment can also play an intrinsic and instrumental role in our education towards social, political and economic justice. Jainism deems all human beings to be equally free to attain higher moral and spiritual growth. They are capable of establishing a non-violent, non-exploitative and just social order. They can achieve personal liberation and social justice by their commitment to no-violence and detachment.

BUDDHISM

Mahatma Buddha was one of the foremost spiritual geniuses of human history. He assembled a very radical critique of Hindu metaphysics, theology and axiology. While Buddha was critical of Hindu metaphysical and theological orthodoxy, he did not advance any metaphysical or theological system of his own. He emphasised on ethical teachings leading to the attainment of liberation, which is a state of mind or being, he designated as *Nirvana*. Man is capable of achieving *Nirvana* by recourse to series of trances. This state of being is beyond language, logic and methodology. We can realise *Nirvana* through absolute desirelessness. *Nirvana* is beyond passions and emotions, likes and dislikes, prejudices and impulses etc. At the stage of *Nirvana* all our sorrows are fully fizzled out. Our rational categories of understanding cannot capture the supra-intellectual Wisdom of *Nirvana*. *Nirvana* is identified with Buddhahood. It is mystical union with the Buddha Nature and a realisation of Buddha Wisdom.

Buddha's quest for *Nirvana* was inspired by his profound engagement with human suffering. His intense spiritual investigations led him to an exploration of Four Noble truths:

(1) There is suffering.

(2) The suffering is caused by desires.

(3) We can eliminate suffering by recourse to complete desirelessness.

(4) There is way to stop suffering.

The famous eightfold path of Buddha is the way to stop suffering:

(1) Right views. (2) Right intention. (3) Right speech. (4) Right actions. (5) Right livelihood. (6) Right effort. (7) Right awareness. (8) Right concentration.

In order to achieve *Nirvana*, one has to practise these eight vows, realise the insubstantiality of *Atman* and appreciate the critical salience of Dependent Origination. *Nirvana* is Ultimate Enlightenment. At this stage, our desirelessness leads to sufferinglessness.

Buddha discussed suffering everywhere. The entire ocean of human existence is brimming with suffering. It is our desires which lead to suffering. In order to liberate ourselves from suffering, we have to control desires. We have these innumerable desires; desire for power, desire for property and desire for pleasure. We want to lord over others, maximize our possessions and proliferate our pleasures. In view of these desires, there is violence and injustice. If we want to restore peace and justice, we need to have right views, cultivate right intention, cultivate right speech, carry out right actions, earn right livelihood, make right efforts, have right awareness and appropriate right concentration. It is through practice of these vows that we can achieve desirelessness, leading to elimination of suffering and establishment of peace and justice. A peaceful and just social, political and economic order is possible through our intense moral and spiritual endeavours (Eliade, 1987, Vol. X, p. 241).

1.3 EAST ASIAN TRADITIONS

The Chinese philosophers or thinkers have largely been interested in questions pertaining to society, economy and morality. Take, for example, the case of Taoism. The Chinese sage Lao-Tze underlined certain beliefs or prescribed certain rules of conduct which constitute Tao or way of life. According to Taoism, the world we live in is characterized by two aspects known as *Yin* and *Yan*. These aspects are antithetical and yet complementary, just like sun-shine and shade. Taoism is anchored on the principle of unity. It does not emphases on discursive knowledge which orients man to multiplicity. In order to be unified in Tao, human soul ought to embrace unity which is possible of appropriation by recourse to highest possible mystical experience.

Though deeply mystical, Taoism is also engaged with moral, political and social questions. To be Taoist is to be a man in order of virtue. The ultimate aim of a Taoist is to participate in Universal Consciousness. Any person can participate in such consciousness by recourse to appropriate intellectual transformation. Such an intellectual transformation is vouchsafed to a person who is competent to live by the imperatives of Tao. There is an endless communication going on between the external world and the internal consciousness of man. A Taoist can work out an abiding union will the internal world, for all natural processes are tethered on Tao. An enlightened Taoist can also accomplish harmony with nature. Such a harmonious mode of life can also lead to justice, fairness, righteousness and egalitarianism at social, political and economic levels (Eliade, 1987, Vol. XIV, p.289).

Confucianism has always underlined the significance of social, political, economic and ethical concerns. More importantly, it has emphasized on communitarian morality. It has always aimed at achieving organic unity of the society. In order to achieve such a unity, it has emphasized on the cultivation of filial, piety, mutual love and respectfulness. It is through filial unity that we can manifest our cosmic unity with heaven and earth. It is through cultivation of such a unity that social, political and economic harmony can be achieved and justice and fairness for all can be ensured. Confucianism has placed overwhelming emphasis on cultivation of harmony in social, political and economic spheres of operation (Eliade, 1987, Vol. IV, pp. 15-16).

Japanese people follow or are oriented to Kami. It is a divinely sanctioned world-view and value-system. Faith in the mysterious power of the Kami is the fundamental orientation of Japanese Shintoists. It is beyond language or logic to bring out the essence of Kami which is ineffable. Kami is beyond the category of human understanding. It is only through authentic devotion that we can grasp the Will of Kami. The attunement to Kami can be accomplished by true, sincere and upright human beings. We can achieve communion with Kami and the blessings of Kami through appropriate spiritual struggle leading to purification of thought. Only such a spiritual struggle can lead to social, political and economic justice (Eliade, 1987, Vol. XIII, pp. 287-288).

ZOROASTRIANISM

The fundamental belief of Zoroastrianism is that there is an eternal conflict between *Ohrmazd* and *Ahriman* or the principle of Good and principle of Evil. Human life is characteristically on the horns of this dilemma. The human moral struggle consists in putting up fight against evil and submitting to the principles of righteous or religious life. Man has the ability to be responsible, to abide by moral principle and to surrender to the principles of righteousness. It is man's duty to uphold virtue and justice.

Zoroastrians understand their religion as the word of God. Zoroastrianism is an expression of the Divine Wisdom or Divine Mind. Religion is word of God. Such a word of God has to operate on earth within a definite social structure. In ancient Persia, it operated in the social hierarchy constituting the Sassanian Empire. Both the Zoroastrian religion and the Sassanian Empire were born of one womb. They mutually reinforced each other (Naidoo,1989, p. 29). The political power of the King was sustained by *Ohrmazd* who appoints the King or Emperor to govern in royal righteousness. Such a rule has to conform to all prescriptions of justice for all men. Under such a rule powerful would not exploit the weak. The weaker sections of the people had the right to ventilate their grievances by recourse to religious law. It was the religious duty of the King or Emperor to establish the rule of law, thereby providing justice to every human being.

Zoroastrian religion holds that justice is the right of all human beings irrespective of their religious faith or cultural heritage. Zoroastrianism underlined religious tolerance and pluralism since its very beginning. Zoroastrians insisted on religious harmony and common human welfare and were devoid of any evangelical concern for conversion.

1.4 GREEKS

The pre-Socrates philosophers were mostly concerned with ontological and cosmological questions. The Sophists, just before Socrates, did ask questions pertaining to knowledge, truth and virtue. However, the philosophers who were profoundly interested in the exploration of virtue were Socrates, Plato and Aristotle. The Greeks in general, looked upon justice as 'virtue in actions'. To them justice was the virtue of the soul and injustice was the vice of the soul (Bhandari, 2002, p. 5).

Plato and Aristotle deemed justice to be goodness as well as readiness to follow Laws. Justice signified correspondence of rights and duties. It signified the ideal of profession in the context of human relationships. To Greeks, justice signified the spirit to discharge one's duty. Justice implied balance and harmony in thought and action. The following words represent Greek conception of justice:

> The Greeks were devoted to their laws partly because of the belief in their superhuman origin and partly because the general principles embodying the law were believed to be perfect and permanent, not subject to change at the will of the people. Nature was the source of law and the duty of the State was ordinarily considered to be the application rather than the creation of the law. Law, to the Greeks, was moral because it was natural and, therefore, it constituted the cement of the City-State. Law was the same for all and, therefore, in a way, it meant freedom. Obedience to laws was an essential element in the Hellenic conception of liberty (Ibid, pp. 4-5).

For the Greeks:

> The City-State was both a Church as well as a political institution, and its end was to promote among its citizens goodness, and justice, the latter representing an ideal perfection in human relationships (Ibid, p. 2).

PLATO

Plato was powerfully impacted by Socrates who asked profound questions with regard to knowledge, truth, goodness and justice etc. Under the impact of Socrates, Plato also regards justice as the true principle of social life (Barker, 1952, p. 153). In view of the same, Plato named his most important work, 'Republic' as a discussion on justice.

Plato was a keen observer of his contemporary social, political and economic conditions. He saw people in the City-States to be pitted against one another. Societies were rampantly unrighteous and the States were incorrigibly unjust (Wayper, 1954, p. 16). He saw ignorance masquerading as knowledge (Ibid, p. 16). Socrates had been killed in Athens before his very eyes. Apart from ignorance, the politics of the City-States was dominated by selfishness. Plato yearned for harmony in place of selfishness and civil discord. Plato addressed his Republic to the achievement of such a harmony. He was fully convinced that unless such fundamental political evils of the day such as incompetence and factionalism were not addressed, the City-States cannot be restored back to normalcy and propriety (Sabine, 1949, p. 52). In short, Plato was convinced that the health of the City-States can only be restored by recourse to justice.

Plato discovers and locates justice with help of his Ideal State. He reviews various stages in the development of the conception of justice and morality and also re-examines various theories of justice.

Plato's Republic does not sketch out a fictitious State or an imaginary State. Plato's aim is to found a State on his celebrated theory of ideas. According to Plato, his State is not unreal; it is the only real State. In fact, the reality of his State is the ground of existence of all other existing States.

The State can be justified only if it is founded on rational, real, objective, substantial, eternal, universal and transcendental ideas. Only such a State can be deemed worth establishing. The statecraft has to be rational. It cannot be driven by impulses and interests. It has to be founded on highest rational or philosophical standards. Only philosophers as rational beings can be entrusted with State-craft. Other classes in the society such as warriors and labourers cannot direct the State. The State can be run only on rational standards. Warriors can defend the State from the internal rebellion and external aggression. The labourers or masses have to play a very important economic role in the society. They have to engage in agriculture, industry, business and commerce. However, it is philosophers who can play the role of rulers or leaders.

Of course, philosophers have the far more significant role of contemplating the world of ideas. They cannot be asked to play a political role unless the State is run according to highest rational philosophical standards. Therefore, the State has to be run by rational standards of application, administration and evaluation. The philosophers will have to play the role of rulers. Ideally speaking, their far more honourable function is to contemplate the world of ideas. However, establishment of rational State is absolutely essential for the attainment of virtue, happiness, perfection and justice. Therefore, the philosophers will have to unavoidably shoulder the responsibility of presiding over the State. Philosophers are blessed with wisdom. Warriors are bestowed with courage. The masses or workers share the appetitive part of the soul. In view of the same, they need to cultivate temperance or self-control. A harmonious interaction of wisdom, courage and self-control will lead to justice. Thus, we can establish a just society or State.

Plato held that soul is essentially rational and immortal. The source of the goodness of soul is the world of ideas which is the world of true Beings. Human body is material and is the source of all evils. It is a kind of temporary prison-house. Liberation from the body and contemplation of the beautiful realm of ideas is the ultimate aim of life. Human soul is characterised by reason, courage and appetite. The impulses of the wise soul are ruled by reason. The soul is brave if its spirited part is obedient to the rational part. The soul is temperate if both spirit and appetite are dictated by reason. However, if all the three parts of the soul perform their functions in unison, the soul is just. A man attains to self-realization if he is wise, courageous, temperate and just. The harmony of the soul attained by the exercise of the four virtues such as wisdom, courage, temperance and justice is the highest good of life. Those who attain such a highest good, achieve greatest happiness through the contemplation of highest ideas (Weber, 2000, p. 73). Plato deems justice to be fundamental virtue or mother of all virtues. These virtues belong to various aspects of the soul. With reference to reason, wisdom is the justice; with reference to courage, the will-power is the justice and with reference to appetite, temperance is the justice. In our relationship with Deity, piety is the justice. To be just is the essence of morality. Man's way to self-realization and God-realization is justice. The realization of justice is possible only in the State. The State is like the collective man or an individual on the large scale. In view of the same, individual interest must be merged in the collective interest. The individual must live for the family and the family must live for the State. All the children belong to the State which is like one large family. The State is the parent as well as the teacher of the children. Justice for Plato signifies a principle of non-interference; the various classes of the society are to be kept within their limits. Various individuals of a class are to be kept in their limits and various elements in an individual soul are to be kept within limits. Justice is ruling virtue and integrates other virtues such as wisdom, courage and self-control within their appropriate limits. The presiding virtue of the justice integrates the entire society (Bhandari, 1963, pp. 21-22).

ARISTOTLE

In his 'Nichomachean Ethics' Book V, Aristotle works out an analysis of justice. For Aristotle, justice is what is lawful and fair. A lawless person according to Aristotle is unjust and a law-abiding man is just. All lawful acts are just acts (Ross, 2003, p. 98).

The just is what's lawful and fair and unjust is what's unlawful and unfair (Ibid). Justice signifies lawfulness or fairness. A just person is lawful and virtuous. For Aristotle, justice is complete virtue in its fullest sense. A person who possesses justice can exercise all other virtues and can benefit not only himself but also others. Every virtue as exercised for the good of the community is simultaneously an act of justice.

For Aristotle, justice in the broad sense is known as universal justice. Universal justice emanates from law-abidingness; for laws in the opinion of Aristotle address all matters, they aim at advantage of all the people and they produce, preserve, and ensure happiness for the entire community. However, Aristotle's conception of universal justice as law-abidingness can be subjected to critical appraisal. It can be pointed out that justice as law-abidingness cannot provide a standard of what is just. It is always not the case that in order to be just we should obey the law. It may be that by obeying the law we may be doing what's unjust. We may sometimes disobey the law and yet our actions may be just. Thus, Aristotle complements his universal justice by another conception of justice known as particular justice. The particular justice is subdivided into two types, (1) Distributive justice and (2) Rectificatory or Remedial or Corrective justice. Distributive justice has reference to distribution of honour, status, property, money, or other things that are to be divided among share-holders. In such a distribution, there is always the possibility of someone getting larger share or less then what is due to him or her (Ibid, 102). Distributive justice entails distribution of profits and losses, benefits and burdens and wealth and honour fairly among the citizens of a society. As against distributive justice, rectificatory justice remedies unequal distribution of profit and loss between genuine share-holders. It is by recourse to remedial or corrective justice that we attempt to restore fairness and balance in the distribution of goods and honours. We require corrective justice in case any member of a community has been burdened or benefitted with more or less than what's deserved by him or her. In view of the same, Aristotle underlines that each one of us should get ones due share from social distributions and in case anyone is wronged, he or she should be appropriately compensated. Our rights and remedies have reference to law and correspondingly justice signifies determination of rights and remedies according to the provisions of law.

The question of justice in relation to the equality is also taken up by Aristotle. He does not accept human equality in the contemporary democratic egalitarian sense. As per the predilections of his time, Aristotle is not convinced that all human beings are equal as human beings.

> Aristotle regards human society as inevitably and naturally hierarchical: he assumes as self-evident that the male's abilities are superior to the female's, and the master's to the slave's and that Greeks are superior to non-Greeks (Sinclair, T.A. 1992, p. 56).

Human inequality is assumed as a natural fact by Aristotle. In view of the same, he assumes that men who are intellectually superior to others, are naturally fit to be the ruling class and the inferior masses are only fit to be ruled by their superiors. Males are superior to the females and therefore, deserve to rule females. Masters are superior to slaves and therefore, fit to rule slaves. The females and slaves are respectively only fit to be ruled by males and masters. Following his master, Plato, Aristotle also holds that society is comprised of three main classes; (1) men blessed with reason and wisdom or philosophers are fit to be rulers, (2) men who are bestowed with courage and are fit to be warriors and (3) vast majority of men who are characterised by appetite only and will have to operate as traders, agriculturists, artisans, labourers or workers. The virtue of the rulers is their wisdom, the virtue of the warriors is the courage and the virtue of the workers is the cultivation of temperance or self-control. It signifies that, according to Aristotle, all human beings are not equally entitled to positions of authority. Only virtuous and wise persons enlightened by reason are entitled to such positions. Aristotle does not deem women, slaves and workers as citizens. They are simply devoid of any entitlement to rule. They are incapable of giving a judgement or holding an office. Women and slaves are simply incapable of holding any office. They are simply excluded from any positions of authority. For Aristotle:

> Citizens are a particular class of men, to which no one who is constantly engaged in commercial or manual labour can belong, at any rate in the 'best' state. Such people simply do not have the time and opportunity to fulfil the essential function of a citizen, to rule (while holding office) (Ibid, p. 183).

Aristotle holds:

> that the state should confer political power, privilege and status in proportion to 'value received', i.e. in proportion to the contribution men

> make to the total purpose for which the state exists, the good life, which entails the exercise of all the distinctly human virtues. Such a distribution would be 'just' in a complete sense... he puts good birth and ownership of property on the list, and the moral qualities of justice and courage; a high level of culture and education too will be a token of merit in one who is to take part in the working of a state which aims at securing the good life. Men are not equal in these respects, and any state which ignores this fact and thinks in terms of absolute equality must be one of the wrong types, a 'deviation'. The upper groups will always be superior in education and ability (Ibid, pp. 193-194).

For Aristotle, democracy is the worst form of government, for it deems all human beings to be equal. He considers aristocracy to be the best form of government, for it is in such a system in which a few wise rulers blessed with virtue and wisdom, are entitled to rule.

In view of the same, Aristotle thinks that justice entails equality only for equals. Only equal persons can have equal rights or equal opportunities. For Aristotle, "what is just in distribution must be according to merit" (Ross, 2003, p. 103). He underlines that such goods as wealth, honour, opportunities etc should be distributed in between different individuals in keeping with their merit or worth. Such a view is designated as proportional equality (McKerlie, 2001, p. 139). It signifies that people of greater merit should receive greater share, they cannot have identical shares without any consideration to their merit (Sinclair, 1992, p. 206). In case persons are equal in worth, their shares with regard to relevant goods will be equal. In case they are unequal in worth, their share of relevant goods will also be proportionately unequal. In view of the fact that the most significant contribution to the State is made by the most virtuous people, they are entitled to highest honour. Women, slaves and workers are incapable of making any contribution to the affairs of the State. Accordingly, they are the least virtuous people and entitled to receive least share, honour and wealth (McKerlie, 2001, p. 119).

Aristotle advocates that social reciprocity among the citizens should be proportional rather than equal. No one should unfairly get less and no one should unfairly get more. There should be proportional equality. For Aristotle, the justice is in proportion and the violation of proportion is injustice.

Aristotle's principle of justice is anchored on merit or virtue. On the basis of this principle, Aristotle justifies inequality among Greeks and non-Greeks, slaves and masters as well as males and females. However, his theory of justice is not fair. He discriminates on the basis of race, gender and ethnicity. Aristotle could not understand that if women, workers and non-Greeks are provided opportunities, they can also prove their worth and make significant contribution to the affairs of the state. Thus, Aristotle fails to provide a balanced account of human rights without any regard to situational or circumstantial contingencies. Like his master Plato, Aristotle fails to respect all persons as free and rational agents.

REFERENCES

1. Kessler, P. (2000). *The Jewish Concept of Justice. The Way Supplement*, 91.

2. Dunning, W. A. (1966). *Political Theories – Ancient and Medieval.* Vol. I, Allahabad: Copyright.

3. Krause, P. (2018). *Augustine on Love, Justice, and Pluralism in Human Nature.* See also Augustine, *City of God.* 19.4. (https://www.printfriendly.com/p/g/t6PFAZ).

4. Sharma, C. D. (1987). *A Critical survey of Indian Philosophy.* Delhi: Motilal Banarsidass.

5. Mahadevan, T. M. P. (1974). *Invitation to Indian Philosophy.* New Delhi: Arnold Publisher.

6. Eliade. M. (1987). *The Encyclopedia of Religion.* Vol. IV, X, XIII, XIV, Macmillan.

7. Naidoo, T. (1989). *Human Rights: a Zoroastrian Perspective.* Journal for the study of Religion 2, (2).

8. Bhandari, D. R. (2002). *History of European Political Philosophy.* Bangalore: Bangalore Press.

9. Barker, E. (1952). (4th edition). *Greek Political Theory – Plato and His Predecessors.* London.

10. Wayper. C. L. (1954). (1st edition). *Political Thought.* English Universities Press Ltd.

11. Sabine, G. H. (1949). (3rd edition). *A History of Political Theory.* UK: George Harrap.

12. Weber, A. (2000). *History of Philosophy.* Translated by Thilly, F. India: Surjeet Publication.

13. Aristotle: *Nichomachean Ethics.* (1980). Translated by Ross, W. D. New Delhi: Cosmo Publications.

14. Aristotle: *The Politics.* (1992). Translated by Sinclair, T. A. London: Penguin Books Ltd.

15. McKerlie, D. (2001). Aristotle's theory of justice. *The Southern Journal of philosophy* 39(1).

CHAPTER-II

QUR'ĀNIC CONCEPT OF JUSTICE

2.1 DEFINATION OF JUSTICE IN ISLĀM

The question of justice has been central to all ancient, medieval and modern social, political, economic, ethical and philosophical accounts. The problem of justice has also been central to Islāmic theology, philosophy, ethics, politics, law etc.

The word 'justice' 'in Arabic language' is translated as *'Adl'* which signifies balance, equity, fairness, equality, detachment etc. In Mu'tazilism and Shī'ahism, *'Adl'* or Divine justice is deemed to be one of their fundamental principles. Abdul Rashid Numani in his *Lughat al-Qur'ān* defines *'Adl'* to mean balance, equity, proportion, compensation etc. (Numani, 1986, pp. 247-249). According to Al-Mawardi, *'Adl'* means moral and religious perfection (Gibb, 1979, p. 209). According to Maulana Maūdudī *'Adl'* means balance in interpersonal human rights. It also means balance in rights of God towards man. Furthermore, it also signifies a balance between right and wrong. According to Maūdudī *'Adl'* does not mean equality, it means to give one his due (Maududi, 2014, p. 442).

Muslim political philosophers, theologians, jurists, etc have tried to define justice from time to time. However, these definitions have been too comprehensive and imprecise to provide any exact understanding of justice. In view of the same, the renowned Muslim philosopher Malki jurist Ibn Rushd has observed that it has never been possible to arrive at a consensual definition of the term *'Adl'*. More often than not, justice has been interchangeably used with goodness. A good person is just person. It can also be said that an individual person must cultivate goodness. However, at societal or political plane, we must strive for social, political, and economic justice. Even 'goodness' has definitely a social, political and economic connotation. Normally, all human beings pursue their own interests. However, to be good signifies to be good to others, to be cognizant of their rights, to strive for their welfare, to direct them towards education and skill development with a view to making them responsible and independent citizens of any Society or State. In view of the same, we can say that goodness and justice are integrally connected at the semantic plane (Gibb, 1979, p. 209).

Adl or Justice in the Arabic language and Islāmic discourse can have numerous connotations and contexts. It can mean doing things in certain ratio proportion. For example, we have to use scores of items, ingredients, components and elements in a certain proportion with a view to building a house. Thus, to be just means to be proportionate. Justice, equity, or equality etc, do operate within a certain legal and constitutional contexts. Justice means equality and equal human rights in a constitutional context in which all people irrespective of caste, creed and color do have equal rights and duties. Justice, in context of Islām, does mean observance of individual rights. Allah asks people to be just towards one another. He also commands to judge between human beings justly. Justice signifies obedience to the commandments of Allah. Establishment of justice has been counted as one of the purposes of divine revelations.

The most common word for justice is '*adl*'. There are other several synonyms of '*adl*' such as *qist, qasd, istiqama, nasib, hissa, mizan* etc. The antonym of *adl* is '*jawr*'. The word '*jawr*' has also several synonyms such as '*zulm*' (wrongdoing), *tughyan* (tyranny), *mayl* (inclination), *inhiraf* (deviation) etc. The word '*adl*' is an abstract noun derived from '*adala*' which means to strengthen, to sit straight, to run away from one (wrong path) to the other the (right path). It can also mean to 'balance, to 'weigh' or to be in a state of 'equilibrium'. Something which is not upright is deemed to be *jawr* or unfair. Thus, straightforwardness and uprightness are the equivalents of justice. *Adl* signifies something or some action that is right and *jawr* signifies something or some actions that is wrong. Any action carried out within the limits of moral and religious values is *adl*. Thus, *adl* signifies fairness and equitableness as well. *Adl* also signifies equality before law and equal rights for all. The principle of distributive justice is expressed by such terms as *nasib* and *qist* (share) and *qistas* and *mizan* (Khadduri, 1984, PP. 6-7). In its theological context, justice means 'righteousness' 'the observance of the divine law' and 'the state of being just before God'. In its ethical context, justice means 'one of the four cardinal virtues' 'the just conduct or the quality of being just and the principle of just dealing, in its legal context, justice means 'exercise of authority or power in the maintenance of right, vindication of right by assignment of reward or punishment, infliction of punishment, legal vengeance on an offender, in its social context, justice means 'to render what is one's due, vindicate one's just claims, to do something in a manner worthy of one's abilities, etc (Qureshi, 1982, p. 35).

The Arabic term *Ihsan,* which is closely associated with in Qur'ān can also resolve the problem of *Adle.* The Arabic term *Ihsan* means kindness. Reciprocity also plays a very important role in the form of justice, as God reciprocates good for good, but only if human reciprocates God's kindness with kindness to fellow humans. This idea of reciprocity as a form of justice extends also to actions among humans. In this sense *Ihsan* is understood as defining kindness as a mode of justice in the reciprocal performance of these deeds.

As much as these ideas may have seemed radically new at the time of the proclamation of the Qur'ān, they also must have been in some real ways familiar. Confronted with dual limitations of language and history, the Qur'ān was forced to express these new ideas within old semantic frameworks. And while some terms achieve a wholesale redefinition, in most cases, words never quite lose their previous meanings and connotations. The Qur'ānic vocabulary of justice embraces this indeterminacy to paint as rich and as thick a definition as possible, elevating previously only quasi-ethical indicative terms, to the level of primary value terms.

Ma'rūf explicitly reveals this semantic dilemma, simultaneously affirming and rejecting the pre-Islāmic ethical framework. While *ma'rūf* implies that what is "known" is just, it does so within the limits of the Qur'ān itself, demanding justification beyond the presumed justness of custom and tradition. It is only the revealed word of God that characterizes *ma'rūf* as justice. Thus, even as *ma'rūf* seems to affirm the idea of an ethical-continuity with the pre-Islāmic era, it forces a fundamental reorientation of the ethical concept of justice such that becomes an "ethico-religious" concept, dependent on God for meaning.

The root *qṣt* and 'dl, which had not been properly ethical in the pre-Islāmic era, had certainly carried positive connotations. The former represented a virtue in the marketplace, expressing fair scales and fair dealing. The latter would have been associated with life in the desert, standing for the straightness, and hence relative ease, of one's trek across the peninsula. The Qur'ān adopted these ideas and redeployed them in are religious, and hence ethical, context in order to underpin the Qur'ānic conception of justice.

However the Qur'ān never unifies these ethical ideals into a singular idea of justice, but rather constructs justice as a field of concepts. This field is anchored on the one hand by the imperative to imitate God, embodied by the divine "fair-dealing" of *qṣt* that the Qur'ān demands humans seek to emulate. On the other hand the pastoral imperative represented by *'adl* establishes communal solidarity as equally important in the Qur'ānic construction of justice. While the two ideas are qualitatively different, their significant overlap is evident in the idea of *iḥsān*, which represents justice, through kindness, as the simultaneous fulfilment of the pastoral and divine-mimetic ethical imperatives (Bernstein, 2009, pp. 65-67).

There is no perfect or absolute definition of justice. Any concept of justice evolves out of given historical, cultural, social, political and economic conditions of a given society. Justice is always relative to an established public order, which public order establishes a certain scale of justice. Our scales of justice vary from place to place and from time to time.

2.2 THE QUR'ĀN ON JUSTICE

It goes without saying that the Qur'ān most emphatically underlines justice, equity, equality, fairness, rectitude etc. Any reader of the Qur'ān can easily discern the Qur'ānic emphasis on such values as justice, equity, equality, fairness etc. The Qur'ān emphasizes that all human beings have been created from one source:

> O, people! Be careful of your Lord, who created you from a single being (*Al-Qur'ān*: 7:189).

> We have honored the sons of Adam; provided them with transport on land and sea; given them for sustenance things good and pure; and conferred on them special favors, above a great part of Our Creation (Ibid, 17:70).

> O mankind! We created you from a single (pair) of a male and a female, and made you into nations and tribes, that ye may know each other (not that ye may despise each other). Verily the most honored of you in the sight of Allah is (he who is) the most righteous of you. And Allah has full knowledge and is well acquainted (with all things) (Ibid, 49:13).

These verses indicate that the Qur'ān does not allow us to differentiate between the people on grounds of culture, language, class, caste, creed, colour, etc. Justice demands that each human is treated on equal footing. Every person is honourable as a human being. Every other consideration or distinction pales into insignificance.

Apart from human equality, the Qur'ān also lays emphasis on cultivation of moderation. The Qur'ān declares Muslims as a community on middle path so that they can be the bearers of witness to the people. While adopting any social, political and economic course of action, Muslims should not commit any excess or deficiency in theory or action. They should adopt the middle way of solving problems with a view to maintaining balance. Muslims need to cultivate moderation in order to establish a just social, political and economic order.

Islām declares man to be Allah's vicegerent and in view of this office he cannot escape or run away from his responsibility and accountability. The Prophet is reported to have said that every human being is caretaker and accountable for what has been assigned to him (Qureshi, 1982, p. 38). It is obligatory on everyone to deal with all matters under one's consideration with equity and justice. In case, there is conflict between our individual interests and collective goals, we should side with the latter. The following verse of the Qur'ān illustrates the same:

> Allah doth command you to render back your Trusts to those to whom they are due; and when ye judge between man and man, that ye judge with justice: Verily how excellent is the teaching which He giveth you! For Allah is He Who heareth and seeth all things (*Al-Qur'ān*: 4:58).

This verse of the Qur'ān indicates that individuals should get assignments or projects for which they have a natural aptitude. While entrusting responsibilities or official positions, the public institutions should ascertain the suitability of the candidates overlooking their personal desires and preferences. Furthermore, the implementation of an ideal society and establishment of peace and justice entail solidarity and cooperation. The Qur'ān makes such cooperation obligatory on believers: "And help one another in righteousness and piety and help not one another in sin and aggression, and keep your duty to Allah" (Ibid, 5:3). It means that interpersonal cooperation is essential for the establishment of a just society. The believers should cooperate for purposes that are good and not evil. The Qur'ān asks Muslims not to wrong others nor allow yourself to be wronged by others. "Deal not unjustly, and ye shall not be dealt with unjustly" (Ibid, 2:279).

The Qur'ān repeatedly underlines the significance of justice in all spheres of human operation. Most importantly it exhorts Muslims never to exploit people socially, politically or economically; rather it asks Muslims to strive for social, political and economic justice. Accordingly, the Qur'ān prohibits Muslims to discriminate on grounds of caste, colour, and creed (Ibid, 49:13).

In the interest of social, political and economic justice, Islām accords equal fundamental rights to all. It promises to protect life, property and honour of every citizen. It also protects the personal freedom of every citizen. According to the Prophet of Islām, unless a specific charge against a person cannot be proved, such a person cannot be imprisoned or detained (Qureshi, 1982, p. 82). The Second Caliph of

Islām Umar is reported to have said, "In Islām no one can be imprisoned except after proper judicial inquiry" (Imām Malik, p. 2:720 (Kitab al- Aqdiyah), Cairo 1951). Islām also accords freedom of opinion and belief. The Qur'ān underlines that there is no compulsion in religion.

> Let there be no compulsion in religion: Truth stands out clear from Error: Whoever rejects Evil and believes in Allah hath grasped the most trustworthy handhold, that never breaks. And Allah heareth and knoweth all things. (*Al-Qur'ān*:2:256).

Islām also accords the right to basic necessities of life to all the citizens without any discrimination. All citizens have also right to equal opportunities without any regard to social and political rank.

According to Islām, Allah has appointed human beings as His vicegerent. Each human being is vicegerent of Allah. Any person belonging to any culture, history, geography, caste, Colour, ethnicity etc, is entitled to being appointed as Ruler, Caliph, Imām, *Ameer* etc. provided that he believes in the unicity of Allah, authenticity of the Prophet Muhammad and the veracity of the eschatological accountability on the Day of Judgement and most importantly is pious and God-fearing. Allah has promised believers to grant them vicegerency in the land just as He made others before them to succeed at appropriate stages of history.

> Allah has promised, to those among you who believe and work righteous deeds, that He will, of a surety, grant them in the land, inheritance (of power), as He granted it to those before them; that He will establish in authority their religion—the one which He has chosen for them; and that He will change (their state), after the fear in which they (lived), to one of security and peace: 'They will worship Me (alone) and not associate aught with Me.' If any do reject Faith after this, they are rebellious and wicked (Ibid, 24:55).

This verse illustrates that Sovereignty belongs to Allah and believers have been promised to be appointed as vicegerents. Under ideal or normal conditions, it is not possible to monopolise political power all individual believers are entitled to directly or indirectly participate in politics and decide their socio-political powers. The leaders of the community in consultation with one another will elect head of the State in the light of Qur'ānic guidance viz; "They manage their affairs by mutual consultation" (Ibid, 42:38), "And take consultation with them in affairs" (Ibid, 3:159). All believers are equal before Islāmic *Sharī'ah*. All believers are asked to cultivate the best of intentions, to strive for good (*Khayr*), to give up evil *(Sharr),* to abide by what is

Divinely prescribed and normally acceptable *(Maruf)* and to refrain from doing what is Divinely proscribed and normally unacceptable *(Munkar)*. God asks believers to maintain justice and bear the witness for the sake of Allah.

> O ye who believe! Stand out firmly for justice, as witnesses to Allah, even as against yourselves, or your parents, or your kin, and whether it be (against) rich or poor: For Allah can best protect both. Follow not the lusts (of your hearts), lest ye swerve, and if ye distort (justice) or decline to do justice, verily Allah is well acquainted with all that ye do. (Ibid, 4:135).

It is obligatory on believers to become witness for justice, even if the judgement goes against believers themselves or their parents or their near relatives or against the rich and poor. The Qur'ān, furthermore, specifically asks believers not to let hatred of people incite you not to act equitably.

> O ye who believe! Stand out firmly for Allah, as witnesses to fair dealing, and let not the hatred of others to you make you swerve to wrong and depart from justice. Be just: That is next to Piety: And fear Allah. For Allah is well acquainted with all that ye do. (Ibid, 5:9).

Those who judge between people, should not commit injustice; come what may, hell or high water.

> Allah doth command you to render back your Trusts to those to whom they are due; and when ye judge between man and man, that ye judge with justice: Verily how excellent is the teaching which He giveth you! For Allah is He Who heareth and seeth all things (Ibid 4:58).

Thus, the Qur'ān establishes the highest standard of justice and only such a standard can serve as the touchstone of a just society.

Islām has advanced an economic system catering to the justice both at individual and social planes. The guiding principle of Islāmic economy is moderation. Islām does not agree with contemporary capitalists to own limitless properties or means and modes of production. Capitalists err on excess, on the other hand, socialistists, by abolishing private ownership, err on deficiency. Islām takes a balanced view of both individual rights and collective responsibilities. It accepts that all men are not physically and mentally equally endowed. Therefore, all individuals are entitled to strive for maximum possible appropriation of land, gold, diamond, silver, money, business etc. However, they cannot have the absolute rights to appropriate to the levels where interests of the common masses cannot be safeguarded. Individual rights cannot be over-stressed. Such a stance can lead to jeopardization of the collective interests of society.

To begin with, we need to understand that Allah repeatedly brings out in the Qur'ān that He is the Absolute Ruler and Owner of this universe including the resources of earth. Man, at best, has been appointed as the vicegerent of Allah. Accordingly, billionaires, trillionaires and zillionaires of the earth cannot claim absolute ownership of all the properties and resources at their disposal. Their ownership rights will finally have to negotiate the following verses of the Qur'ān:

> And Allah's is the treasures of the heavens and earths (Ibid, 63:7).
>
> And Allah's is the dominion of the heaven and earth (Ibid, 5:18).
>
> And there is not a thing but with us are the treasures of it, and we send it not down but in a known measures (Ibid, 15:21).
>
> Whatsoever is in the heavens and in the earth has been subjected to serve your needs (Ibid, 45:12).
>
> Believe in Allah and His Apostle and spend out of what He has made you to be vicegerent (57:7).

Man has been made a vicegerent of Allah. He is a trustee of what has been given to him by his Lord. He cannot spend wealth given to him by his Lord on gratification of personal desires only. He is asked to spend on his needs and what is in excess of his needs he should spend on poor, needy, have-nots, enfeebled apart from spending it on parents, relatives, orphans. The Qur'ān specifically asks Muslims not to create an economic system in which wealth is concentrated in few hands, "so that it may not be a thing taken by turns by among rich of you" (Ibid, 17:100). Furthermore, the Qur'ān asks believers to pay *zakat* and *sadaqat* and also go in for *infaq fi Allah*. The Qur'ān categorically brings out that have-nots have a right on certain portion of the property of haves. "And in their wealth and possessions (was remembered) the right of the (needy,) him who asked, and him who (for some reason) was prevented (from asking)" (Ibid, 51:19).

The Qur'ān also emphasises on the adoption of genuine economic means and modes of production and appropriation of wealth. Thus, it prohibits all illegal commercial activities such as *Ihtikar* (Hoarding), and *Riba* (Usury). In order to fulfil the basic requirements of the poor and needy the government can impose extra taxes. The Qur'ān and the *Sunnah* make it obligatory on haves to cater to the needs of the poor.

In case, the poor people cannot be fed, clothed and housed on the collection of the *Zakat*, the government can impose additional taxes with a view to meeting out their requirements (Qureshi, 1982, p. 49). In fact, the mission of the Islām has been succinctly brought out in the following verse: "Certainly We sent Our messengers with clear arguments, and sent down with them the Book and the measure, that men may conduct themselves with equity" (*Al-Qur'ān:* 57:25).

We can try to understand and define justice from numerous angles of interpretation or perspectives. It can mean placing things in their rightful place. It can be defined to be providing all human beings equal treatment. Justice is intimately linked to equality, as it is through practicing justice that we can create a state of equilibrium. It is through administration of justice that we can distribute rights and duties equitably. Justice is underlined to be one of the supreme virtues by the Qur'ān. The establishment of justice is one of the basic objectives of Islām. In its relevance and significance, justice is next only to faith in the unicity of Allah and faith in the authenticity of the Prophet. In fact, the establishment of justice is the perennial goal of all Divine revelations. The Qur'ān also emphasises that the implementation and execution of justice must be done according to the standards and criteria advanced by the Qur'ān itself. However, one can also discern a latitudinarian approach to justice in Islām. What's crucial or central is the achievement or the attainment of justice. No methods or procedures of achievement of justice have been specifically tabulated by the Qur'ān.

Justice definitely has social, political, economic or institutional connotations. However, the Qur'ān also extends justice to being a personal virtue. Being just is one of the standards of moral excellence. The Qur'ān asks Muslims to be just without any consideration of race, caste, creed, colour, religion, nationality, culture etc. It asks Muslims to be just both to their friends and foes. Justice is one of the attributes of Allah and the Qur'ān underlines that we adopt justice as moral ideal. Administration, establishment and execution of justice is a categorical imperative for a believer in Allah, Prophet and the Qur'ān. The believers should treat each human being with justice and impartiality, for those who judge equitably are lauded by God. The revelations of Allah on the Prophet themselves constitute or embody justice. The Qur'ān itself reveals the balance of right and wrong so that people may stand for justice. Islām teaches absolute, unconditional and categorical significance of justice.

The believers are specifically asked that their hatred for some people should not lead them to transgress the limits of justice. Justice is integral to piety and righteousness and under no circumstances can believers ever afford to depart from the ideal of justice. The Qur'ān also asks believers to be unconditionally true in words and deeds. They should fulfil their promises, commitments and contracts. It is obligatory on Muslims to fulfil their contracts or treaties with people of other faiths, for that is the righteous course of action. The Qur'ān asks believers to establish a system of weights and measurements. They are advised not to skimp in the balance leading thereby to the loss of buyers. Islām categorically prohibits its believers to fraudulently or unjustly appropriate what is due to others. Islām wants maximum possible elimination of mischief upon the earth (Sharif, 2001, pp. 162-163).

Certain societies postulate that human beings are competent of determining their personal or social interests. They are fully cognisant of their needs and aspiration. In view of the same, they are capable of establishing the public order in which a scale of justice can be evolved by recourse to social consensus. Such a concept of justice is born out of an interaction between expectations and existing conditions. Such a notion of justice is definitely imperfect and it is always refined or improved by ongoing processes of social change. Thus, ideal or perfect justice is deemed to be impossible of attainment. However, such a notion of justice is perennially improvised through interminable process of social change. Secondly, there is a social order or setup which is predisposed to thinking that man is essentially incapable of transcending his personal limitations. Our essential human fallibility is innocent of understanding and determining our individual and collective interests. We are morally and spiritually too impoverished or corrupt to lay down an impartial standard of justice. Such a social setup invokes a Superhuman or Divine authority to provide the fundamental principles of public organisation leading to the establishment of a standard of justice. Such a Superhuman authority or Superhuman standard of justice can be exercised and applied by a transcendentally inspired Prophet or chosen believers of the period of revelation. However, such a transcendentally inspired justice can have a perennial or abiding impact on standardisation, evaluation and application of justice. The ancient Hebrews, Christians and Muslims were committed to such an understanding, implementation and administration of justice. The Hebrew, the Christian and the Islāmic version of Semitic world-view and value-system, deemed God to be disclosing Himself through His revelations as well as disclosing a revelatory standard of justice. Such a revelatory standard of justice is deemed applicable to all human situations and institutional mechanisms. In contrast to positive justice advanced by humanistists, this Supernaturally advanced standard of justice may be designated as Divine Justice. Such a standard of justice inspired through intuition and revelation is intimately linked to religion. Such a notion of justice seems to be having closed affinities with Aristotle's account of natural justice. However, Semitic religions such as Judaism, Christianity and Islām visualized and conceptualised justice more in terms of application of Divine Will in human history. While Christians designated the Christian notion of justice as eternal law, the Muslims designated such a notion of justice embodied as *Sharī'ah*. However, Christian and Muslim Scholars have engaged in endless debates with regard to the application, implementation and administration of such justice upon the Earth.

In the Context of Islām, Divine justice is embodied in the Qur'ānic revelations and in the *Sunnah,* the traditions and *Sīrah* of the Prophet. While revelations of Allah are transmitted through Qur'ānic statements, Divine Wisdom is communicated through the sayings and the doings of the Prophets. Thus, the Qur'ān and the Prophet constitute two fundamental textual sources of God's Will and Justice. Muslim theologians and scholars applied human reasoning or *Ijtihad* on these two basic textual sources with a view to laying down law and creed. Thus, Qur'ān, sayings and doings of the Prophet and the creative interpretations and applications of Muslim theologians and scholars form the bedrock of Islāmic public order. Various theories of justice have been advanced by Muslim theologians, scholars and thinkers in the light of textual sources and the inductions and deductions worked out or arrived at by succeeding generations of *Mujatahdin*.

Any theory, standard or scale of justice is relative to its given public order. The Islāmic public order underlines God to be the Sovereign of the community of believers. He is the Ultimate Ruler and Legislator of the community. The Islāmic public order aiming at resolution of the individual and collective problems of the community, is directly rooted in the Revelation and Divine Wisdom. The principles of justice derived from the Qur'ān and *Sunnah* of the Prophet are deemed to be infallible and inviolable. They are designed for all times to come and capable of universal application with a view to resolving all potential and emerging problems at various stages of historical and cultural evolution. The principles of administration, adjudication, implementation and execution derived from Divine Revelation and Divine Wisdom, are ideal and perfect. However, the public order, primarily premised on Divine Laws, is also informed by political activities, judicial interpretations, scholarly rulings and opinions and human inductive and deductive reasoning etc, it is necessarily amenable and adaptable to periodic refinements with a view to meeting out the challenges posed by the changing conditions, intangible situations and imponderable contingencies of the community.

While theoretically accepting God to be the Ultimate Ruler of the community, it was not possible that a direct rule of God over Muslims can be established. It was necessary that some representative of God on Earth be chosen and God's authority be delegated to him. The solution that was arrived at was that no human person or institution can be instituted as the ultimate sovereign of the people, a vicegerent of God could represent Divine Order upon the Earth. In this way a new form of government was established on revealed laws. The government was to be carried out on divinely ordained laws and principles. It was a kind of qualified theocracy in which only the revealed norms of Allah could be deemed to be the locus of political authority.

Muslim theologians, jurists, scholars and thinkers accepted the ultimacy of the Qur'ānic revelations and the Divine Wisdom intimated to the community of believers by the Prophet. All of them agreed that justice is to be administered through these textual sources of Islām. However, all of them did not agree as to how such an.

AFTER LIFE

The Islāmic account of justice is intimately and integrally related with the doctrine of the Day of Judgement. The Qur'ān repeatedly underlines that all human beings will be resurrected on the Day of Judgement. The righteous and pious people will be rewarded with eternal paradisal blessings and vicious people will be sent to hellfire. In fact, faith in the Day of Judgement is the cornerstone of the edifice of Islām. The Qur'ān makes it clear to all human beings that their bad actions will count against them just as their good actions will count for them. The Qur'ān promises that people on the Day of Judgement will be dealt with in accordance with absolute standard of justice and no wrong will be done to anyone. God is aware of all the good and evil done by human beings and every atom of good and evil will be factored into the account of each human being so that justice is carried out with unqualified exactitude. The process of creation has been initiated by Allah and He has repeatedly carried on this process, with a view to ultimately delivering justice to both righteous and unrighteous people on the Day of Judgement.

THE PROPHET

The Prophet Muhammad was the Epitome of Mercy and Justice. He was deeply moved by the all pervasive inequality and oppression in the Arab society. He relentlessly fought for the establishment of socio-political order and harmony leading to the acknowledgment of a distinct standard of justice. As the last Prophet and the seal of the Prophets he was sent by the Almighty for the widespread cultivation of human dignity, education and values. He was a social reformer of the highest order and changed the Arab society and laid the foundation of just and value bound and value oriented society, social order and civilization. His numerous decisions provided inspiration for social reform to the succeeding generations of Muslim community. As an embodiment of uprightness, balance, fairness and wisdom, he was most powerfully driven by social, political and economic quest for justice. He put up insurmountable struggle for the emancipation of the downtrodden masses of Arabia. He undertook progressive legislative measures for the improvement of the status of women. He strove for the emancipation of slaves and abolition of the system of slavery. He categorically prohibited infanticide and other commissions of injustice.

The Prophet introduced *"Mesaq-i-Madina"* with a view to controlling the waywardness of the tribal society and introduced the concept of State. It was meant to constitutionally consolidate peace, justice, freedom, freedom of religion, a just society, rules of coexistence with non-believers etc. It was promulgated with a view to upholding the dignity of human beings. Furthermore, the prophet gave a moral orientation to politics. He underlined that the real Sovereignty vested with God alone. Under such a theological and legal framework, the ruler would have to operate as a vicegerent of Allah and be also elected by recourse to democratic consensus. The Prophet of Islām conquered Mecca and forgave all of them including his worst enemies. In 632 C.E. he delivered his *Khutb-i-Hajjat-ul-Vidah* which is the universal

Charter of human dignity, justice, peace and equality and is a torch for all the humanity to come is as follows:

> O People, lend me an attentive ear, for I know not whether after this year, I shall ever be amongst you again. Therefore, listen to what I am saying to you very carefully and take these words to those who could not be present here today.
>
> O People, just as you regard this month, this day, this city as Sacred, so regard the life and property of every Muslim as a sacred trust. Return the goods entrusted to you to their rightful owners.
>
> Hurt no one so that no one may hurt you. Remember that you will indeed meet your Lord, and that He will indeed reckon your deeds. God has forbidden you to take usury (interest), therefore all interest obligation shall henceforth be waived. Your capital, however, is yours to keep. You will neither inflict nor suffer any inequity. God has Judged that there shall be no interest, and that all the interest due to Abbas ibn Abd'al Muttalib shall henceforth be waived...
>
> Beware of Satan, for the safety of your religion. He has lost all hope that he will ever be able to lead you astray in big things, so beware of following him in small things.
>
> O People, it is true that you have certain rights with regard to your women, but they also have rights over you. Remember that you have taken them as your wives only under a trust from God and with His permission. If they abide by your rights then to them belongs the right to be fed and clothed in kindness. Do treat your women well and be kind to them for they are your partners and committed helpers. And it is your right that they do not make friends with any one of whom you do not approve, as well as never to be unchaste.
>
> O People, listen to me in earnest, worship God, perform your five daily prayers, fast during the month of Ramadan, and offer *Zakat*. Perform Hajj if you have the means.
>
> All mankind is from Adam and Eve. An Arab has no superiority over a non-Arab, nor does a non-Arab have any superiority over an Arab; a white has no superiority over black, nor does a black have any superiority over white; [none have superiority over another] except by piety and good action. Learn that every Muslim is a brother to every Muslim and that the Muslims constitute one brotherhood. Nothing shall be legitimate to a Muslim which belongs to a fellow Muslim unless it was given freely and willingly. Do not, therefore, do injustice to yourselves.
>
> Remember, one day you will appear before God and answer for your deeds. So beware, do not stray from the path of righteousness after I am gone.
>
> O People, no prophet or apostle will come after me, and no new faith will be born. Reason well, therefore, O people, and understand words which I

convey to you. I leave behind me two things, the Qur'ān and my example, the *Sunnah*, and if you follow these you will never go astray.

All those who listen to me shall pass on my words to others and those to others again; and it may be that the last ones understand my words better than those who listen to me directly. Be my witness, O God, that I have conveyed your message to your people (Prophet Muhammad's Last Sermon, 2013, pp. 3-5) (www.Islāmicreligion. com website).

The Prophet of Islām underlined such values as peace, equality, fraternity and justice. He offered the message of light, hope, justice and peace for all. He stood for universal justice without any recourse to any distinction and discrimination. It goes without saying that Islām as embodied in the Qur'ānic revelations and Divine Wisdom, is a religion of peace, harmony and justice. The Qur'ān unequivocally emphasises that killing a person without any justification amounts to the killing of entire mankind. After belief in the unicity of Allah and the authenticity of Prophet, Islām lays greatest emphasis on justice. The Prophet stood for social, political, economic and cultural justice for all. In his emphasis on justice, the Prophet also laid greatest emphasis on human brotherhood, human equality and tolerance. Accordingly, Islām emphasised on the protection of human rights for all without any discrimination. Such values as love, kindness, cooperation, mutuality, sympathy and compassion have also been greatly emphasised in the Islāmic value-system.

2.3 DISTRIBUTIVE JUSTICE IN ISLĀM

The question of justice has been fundamental in all social, political and economic fields of operation. All social, political and economic interactions unavoidably and inevitably entail or presuppose the dimension of justice. Our social, political, economic and even religious and legal institutions and practices derive their legitimacy from a consideration of establishing or administering justice. In case our institutions and practices fail to do justice or are perceived to be unjust, there are murmurings of change. We can appreciate the pervasiveness of our concern for justice even among our daily interactions. Despite heavy theological and ideological reservations and qualifications, there is a universal appreciation for justice and fairness.

Historically speaking, highly advanced social and political thinkers have displayed unqualified concern for justice and fairness. Islām as a world-view and value-system is predominantly concerned with just distribution of wealth and resources. The emphasis of Islām on distributive justice is second only to faith in Allah and Prophethood of Muhammad. Islām lays great emphasis on institutionalization of peace and justice.

Islām has been fundamentally concerned with the question of distributive justice. The Prophet of Islām made the establishment of a fair and just society to be the raison d'être and locus standi of its Prophethood. However, the problem of justice has to be looked at in the context of early Islām during the years of Prophetic rule from 622 upto 632 at Madina and during the years of *Khulfa-e-Rashideen.* During the Prophet's time the most important consideration for the distribution of money/material/ goods was the need of the recipient. Abu Bakr during his short tenure made equality the prime criterion of distribution of resources. His successor the second Caliph, Umar, emphasised on equity or merit of the recipient to be the criterion of the allocation of resources. Accordingly, he made special allocations to the participants in the battle of Badr. He also made special allocations to the members of the Prophet's family. There were other criteria or norms of distribution such as availability of resources, the needs of the recipients, merit of the recipients, the contribution of the recipients to the cause of Islām, the purpose of allocations etc (Khaliq, & Hassan, 2000, p.163).

Take, for example, the question of succession of the Prophet of Islām. There were vital differences of opinions between believers for the choice of the first successor as well as subsequent successors to the Prophet of Islām. The ultimate criteria for the choice of these appointments were the amount of sacrifice for Islām and nearness of the person to the Prophet. The Prophet of Islām had asked for contributions during the period of the battle of Tabuk. Abu Bakr offered all his belongings, Umar offered half of his belongings and Uthman offered one third of his wealth, with a view to supporting the Muslim army. The appointment of these companions of Prophet as heads of State of Madina was also carried out in corresponding order as well.

Firstly, with regard to distributive justice, Islām guarantees fulfilment of the basic needs to all. Contemporary scholars of Islāmic economics have discussed the issue of basic needs fulfilment in great detail. All of them agree that an Islāmic State has to guarantee the fulfilment of the basic needs to all its citizens. They quote from the Qur'ān and *Sunnah*, from the precedents of first four successors of the Prophet and from juristic consensus to support the thesis that an Islāmic State has to guarantee the fulfilment of basic needs of all the members of the Islāmic Republic. While provision of basic needs is essential and unquestionable in an Islāmic State and society, economists of all ideological positions across the spectrum have carried out extensive analysis of the phenomenon of absolute versus relative poverty. The absolute poverty signifies complete destitution; on the other hand, relative poverty is recognized as well as justified, as being an outcome owing to the natural differences in human potentialities, capacities and endeavours. Thus, justice and morality have to necessarily negotiate numerous considerations emanating from individual merit, personal drives, advantages and disadvantages, favourable or unfavourable market conditions and countless intangibles and imponderables. While Islām prescribes or guarantees the fulfilment of basic needs, it does accept the reality of natural inequalities among human beings.

As we try to figure out the salient features of Islāmic economic philosophy, we need to be cognizant of the complexity of the situation. It can be readily admitted that in a highly organised and competitive international economy, we need a business friendly atmosphere, moderate tax structure, latest technological inputs, competent and competitive teams of managers, producers, marketeers, exporters, innovators, planners etc. An Islāmic economic system will also need to be competing with others having best infrastructural facilities, managerial teams and technological upgradation. However, an Islāmic economy cannot be run only by great engineers, technologists, industrialists, directors, innovators etc. An authentic Islāmic economy needs to be informed by Islāmic beliefs and values as well. Those who are working in an Islāmic economic system need to be educated on beliefs and values constituting Islāmic morality and spirituality. While an Islāmic economy has got to be run on such values as competitiveness, proficiency, efficiency, best possible business administration, critical contributions from technologists and engineers etc, however, culturally, ideologically, educationally and spiritually, it has to be rooted in the world-view and value-system of the Qur'ān. Islām does prescribe certain laws and regulations. However, more than legal rules, it depends on exhortations. The battle for social or distributive justice cannot be fought by recourse to legal mechanisms. It has got to be fought in the minds and hearts of the members of an Islāmic society. An economic order cannot be sustained merely on the basis of a legal framework, it has to be sustained and informed by moral and spiritual guidelines repeatedly underlined by the Qur'ān. Islām does prescribe fulfilment of basic needs however it accepts the reality of natural inequalities. However, this acceptance is not unqualified. It checkmates extreme inequalities by recourse to injunctions of moral values. While Islām emphasises on taking care of basic human needs, it does accept merit as a fair standard of resource allocation. Differences in income are deemed to be justifiable if they emanate from personal talent and individual contributions. Resource allocation, salaries and earnings have got to be proportionate to merit and contribution of the people across the spectrum. However, Islām does prescribe that wealth in excess of our needs be spent on the poor and have-nots in exchange of eschatological incentives in terms of spiritual upliftment, divine blessings and good-pleasure of Allah. Thus, Islām encourages economic volunteerism for a better eschatological reward. The following verses of Qur'ān indicate the same:

> It is not righteousness that ye turn your faces towards the East or West; but it is righteousness--to believe in Allah and the Last Day, and the Angels, and the Book, and the Messengers; to spend of your substance, out of love for Him, for your kin, for orphans, for the needy, for the wayfarer, for those who ask, and for the ransom of slaves; to be steadfast in prayer, and to practice regular charity; to fulfill the contracts which ye have made; and to be firm and patient, in pain (or suffering) and adversity, and throughout all periods of panic. Such are the people of truth, the Allah-fearing (*Al-Qur'ān*: 2:177).
>
> And spend of your substance in the cause of Allah, and make not your own hands contribute to (your) destruction; but do good; for Allah loveth those who do good (Ibid, 2:195).
>
> O ye who believe! Spend out of (the bounties) we have provided for you, before the Day comes when no bargaining (will avail), nor friendship, nor intercession. Those who reject Faith--they are the wrongdoers (Ibid, 2:254).
>
> Those who spend (freely), whether in prosperity, or in adversity; who restrain anger, and pardon (all) men; --for Allah loves those who do good (Ibid, 3:134).
>
> Whatever ye shall spend in the Cause of Allah, shall be repaid unto you, and ye shall not be treated unjustly (Ibid, 8:60).
>
> And in their wealth and possessions (was remembered) the right of the (needy,) him who asked, and him who (for some reason) was prevented (from asking) (Ibid, 51:19).

Social and political thinkers have widely pondered over the question of distributive justice or distributive equality. They advanced divergent perspectives on distributive justice and equality. There are people who argue that all people should have equal amounts of income, perks, privileges, rewards, etc without any regard to their merit or contribution. There are others who suggest that human beings have natural differences in their capabilities, attitudes, skill, knowledge etc and therefore it is fair to have a system in which these natural differences are factored into distribution of incomes, rewards and promotions. Equal distribution to all members of a given society would amount to unfairness or injustice.

Islāmic theory of distributive justice entails the principle of equality and fairness. The fundamental assumption of Islāmic socio-political philosophy is that all human beings are equal and accordingly, all rights and duties should be distributed among them equally or equitably. Distributive justice signifies fair distribution of economic resources. Apart from that there should be fair distributions of rights and duties and wealth and honour among all the members of the community. At its core, distributive justice entails justice towards worst-off members or least advantaged members of any given community. Any exercise or operation towards provision of justice to most disadvantaged members of community, necessitates neutralisation or minimisation of existing inequalities among the people. These inequalities are the result of concentration of wealth or accumulation of wealth in a few hands. We can remove social and economic inequalities only by removal of concentration of wealth and fair distribution of wealth among all the members of a given society. It can be readily agreed that social and economic inequalities, upto an extent, are unavoidable. Islām also accepts the natural unequal distribution of wealth on grounds of equity, equitability and fairness. However, by recourse to its own legislative as well as exhortative stipulations, it tries to minimize wide social and economic inequalities, to the extent possible. It is not possible to work out an exact or geometrical distribution of wealth. However, it is not necessary that we live in a society where enrichment of the rich and impoverishment of the poor should go on indefinitely and endlessly. Islām is cognizant of the fact that unnecessarily unfair distribution of wealth leads to unavoidable social conflicts. In order to prevent the concentration of wealth and bridge the gulf between the rich and the poor and ensure justice and fair distribution of economic resources, Islām stipulates certain legislations as well as exhortative or recommendatory guidelines such as payment of *Zakat*, payment of *Ushr*, payment of *Fitr* at the end of Ramadan, payment of charity (*Sadquat)*, prohibition of *Riba* (usury), law of inheritance etc. The Qur'ān asks us to be just towards *Mustazifun* or the weaker sections of the society. The Qur'ān repeatedly underlines that believers should be just in their dealings with the orphans, the needy and the poor. It asks believers to lead a simple need-based life. The rich and the wealthy people are asked by the Qur'ān to fulfil the basic needs of the poor and the destitute. The Qur'ān stipulates a share of the poor and the needy in the wealth of the rich. The following verse of the Qur'ān testifies to the same: "And those in whose wealth is a recognized right, for the (needy) who asks and him who is prevented (for some reason from asking)" (*Al-Qur'ān*:70:24-25).

The Qur'ān specifically stipulates that the rich and the wealthy should spend their wealth for the betterment of the poor, the wealth that is beyond their needs, "They ask thee how much they are to spend; Say: "What is beyond your needs" (2:219).

The Holy Prophet is reported to have said,

> Anyone who possesses goods more than his needs should give the surplus goods to the weak (and poor); and whosoever possesses food more than his needs should give the surplus food to the needy and the destitute (Begum, 2015, p. 94).

ZAKAT

Islām tries to promote social justice and discourage extreme inequalities. The haves are commanded by Allah to spend the excess of their wealth on the needy and the poor. It recommends a code of conduct and provides concrete guidelines with a view to distributing resources for earning the good-pleasure of Allah. For example, Islām prescribes the payment of *Zakat* for ameliorating the social, political and economic conditions of have-nots. Payment of *Zakat* is one of the five pillars of Islām. The establishment of *Zakat* system is aimed at reducing the absolute poverty. The payment of *Zakat* is obligatory on Muslims for it leads to the fulfilment of the basic needs of the deprived sections of human society. According to Islāmic *Sharī'ah*, the following categories are to be entitled to receive financial assistance from the *Zakat* contributions:

1. The destitute (*Fuqara*): people who are poor and who possess more than their basic needs but do not possess wealth equal to *Nisaab*.
2. The poor (*masakeen*): people who are destitute and extremely needy to the extent they are forced to beg for their daily food ration.
3. Those who are deputed by State to collect Zakah (*al-amileen*): people appointed by an Islāmic official authority to collect *Zakat*. In the absence of an Islāmic official authority, Mosques and Islāmic centers can collect the *Zakat* and use it in proper ways.
4. Those whose hearts are to be reconciled (*mu-allafatul-qulub*): persons who have recently accepted Islām and are in need of basic necessities and would benefit from encouragement by Muslims, which would help strengthen their faith.
5. For the emancipation of slaves (*fi-al-riqab*): slaves who are permitted to work for remuneration and have an agreement from their masters to purchase their freedom on payment of fixed amounts.
6. For relieving one from the burden of debt (*al-gharimin*): persons who have a debt and do not possess any other wealth or goods with which to repay. It is conditional that this debt was not created for any un-Islāmic purpose.
7. In the cause of Allah (*fi-sabilillah*): persons who have to carry out an obligatory deed, which has become obligatory on them and subsequently (due to loss of wealth), are unable to complete that obligation.
8. Way farer *(ibn-us-sabeel)*: persons who are travelers and during the course of their journey do not possess basic necessities, through they are well to do at home. They could be given Zakat in order to fulfill travel needs to return home (Imām Khalid, Zakat in Islām: Conceptualization, categorization &Ruling).(http://docplayer.net/35900031-Zakat-in-Islām-conceptualization-categorization-ruling.html).

Zakat is compulsory and anyone who refuses to pay *Zakat* can be prosecuted by the government. The first Caliph, Abu Bakr, declared *jihad* against those who refused to pay the *Zakat*. Given the complexities of present economic operations across the globe, the *Zakat* system needs to be revived by Islāmic societies for taking care of the poor and the needy.

It is very important that we appreciate the crucial role played by the normative standard of distributive justice in contemporary world society. While it cannot be denied that throughout history there has been relentless exploitation and enslavement. Warlords, kings, feudal lords, industrialists, national and multinational corporates have exploited humans from time to time at various stages of history. However, we are primarily interested in the formulation of criteria or standards of distribution with special references to Islām. Theoretically speaking, most of the societies across history and globe have accepted merit or equity as the most important criterion of resource allocation. However, there can be other criteria which need to be considered in any judicious system of allocation. For example, the needs or requirements of a given section or class of society can be one of the standards of resource allocation. Consideration of equality can also be wisely factored into any holistic system of resource allocation. The distribution of resources should not lead to enrichment of already rich people and further impoverishment of already existing poor people of the society. We need also to consider social peace and social harmony as important criteria of resource allocation. Islām accepts individual merit and contribution to be as natural and thus deems equality as an appropriate norm of resource allocation. However, several measures are prescribed by Islāmic *Sharī'ah* with a view to avoiding extreme disparity in wealth. Islām underlines eschatological reward to be an important incentive for the rich to sacrifice for the poor. Thus, Islām provides a spiritual criterion or standard for the distribution of economic or material resources.

ORPHANS

The Qur'ān has repeatedly asked believers to be kind towards orphans. The guardians of the orphans are categorically asked not to devour the property of the orphans. The Qur'ān says: "Those who unjustly eat up the property of orphans, eat up a Fire into their own bodies: They will soon be enduring a blazing Fire" (*Al-Qur'ān*: 4:10)."Therefore, treat not the orphan with harshness" (Ibid, 93:09).

The Qur'ān commands that the guardians should manage the property of the orphans in best possible manner. They should manage it till the orphans are mature enough to manage it themselves. The following is the warning given by Allah in the *Surah An'am*:"And come not nigh to the orphan's property, except to improve it, until he attains the age of full strength; give measure and weight with (full) justice" (Ibid, 6:152).

Again, the guardians are warned by the Qur'ān not to dissipate the property of orphans, while they are immature and cannot manage it by themselves. The following verse underlines the need for equity and justice in this regard:

> Make trial of orphans until they reach the age of marriage; if then ye find sound judgment in them, release their property to them; but consume it not wastefully, nor in haste against their growing up. If the guardian is well off, let him claim no remuneration, but if he is poor, let him have for himself what is just and reasonable. When ye release their property to them, take witnesses in their presence: But all sufficient is Allah in taking account (Ibid, 4:6).

The Qur'ān asks the guardians of the orphans not to consume the property of orphans unjustly. They should not spend it unfairly or exchange the good property of orphans with their bad property. Those who commit such acts commit great sins. Allah warns them of an eternal punishment for such shameful deeds. The Qur'ān states:

> To orphans restore their property (when they reach their age), nor substitute (your) worthless things for (their) good ones; and devour not their substance (by mixing it up) with your own. For this is indeed a great sin (Ibid, 4:2).

In the above verses embodied into *Surat al-ma'un,* it is clearly brought out that those who do not treat orphans well or do not take care of the needy, are outside the pale of Islām. There are people who offer regular prayers but are unmindful of needs of the poor, their prayers are just a show off and they are not sincerely committed to imperatives of the Qur'ān or commandments of Allah. Prophet Muhammad is reported to have said that feeding a hungry widow is more meritorious than praying whole night. Abu Hurairah reported that the Prophet said: "One who strives for the widows and the poor is like one who fights in the way of Allah" (Karim, 2006, p. 264).

ACCUMULATION OF WEALTH

The accumulation of wealth is condemned by the Qur'ān in the following words:

> O ye who believe! There are indeed many among the priests and anchorites, who in falsehood devour the substance of men and hinder (them) from the Way of Allah. And there are those who buy gold and silver and spend it not in the Way of Allah: Announce unto them a most grievous penalty—"On the Day when heat will be produced out of that

(wealth) in the Fire of Hell, and with it will be branded their foreheads, their flanks, and their backs. –"this is the (treasure) which ye buried for yourselves: Taste ye, then, the (treasures) ye buried! (*Al-Qur'ān*:9:34-35).

The purpose or objective of the Qur'ān is to achieve social justice by recourse to distribution of wealth. It lays emphasis on compulsory payment of *Zakat* and voluntary charity with a view to ameliorating the social and economic conditions of the least advantaged sections of the society

2.4 POLITICAL JUSTICE IN ISLĀM

There are various interpretations with regard to the origin of the State as well as the raison d'être, locus standi and modus operandi of the State. There are political philosophers who deem State to be a natural institution born out of natural evolution. For some, State is highest manifestation of the rational will of man. Some modern European philosophers have advanced Social Contract theory of the State. Semitic theological philosophers have always maintained that a State must be an expression of the Sovereign Will of God through His Prophets and their Successors. Take for example, the following verse of the Qur'ān:

> O David! We did indeed make thee a vicegerent on earth: So judge thou between men in truth (and justice): Nor follow thou the lusts (of thy heart), for they will mislead thee from the Path of Allah (*Al-Qur'ān*: 38:26).

Muslims consider State as the Public order emanating from an Ultimate Superhuman Power or Allah. Muslims as believers were profoundly committed to the doctrine that the State as an expression of public order and justice was derived from high Divine source. On the terrestrial plane, that ultimate source is the Revelation and Wisdom i.e. the Qur'ān and the Prophet's *Sunnah*. These two sources constituted the primary or textual sources of the Islāmic public order or State. All forms of justice proceed from the commandments of Allah who is vested with ultimate Sovereignty. Of course, His Sovereign Will is not exercised directly upon the community of believers. It is exercised through the Prophet and his right guided Caliphs *(Khulafa-i-Rashidin)* who succeed him. The believers are asked to observe the injunctions or commandments prescribed in the Qur'ān and be obedient to the representatives of God who are to judge among men with justice. Their assignment is to exercise God's Sovereign Will on Earth. The Qur'ān exhorts us:

> O ye who believe! Obey Allah, and obey the Apostle, and those charged with authority among you. If ye differ in anything among yourselves, refer it to Allah and His Apostle (Ibid, 4:59).

The Prophet of Islām was granted the power to exercise or implement the Sovereign Will of Allah. The Prophet was commanded by Allah to rule in keeping with the 'truth' and the 'path of God' (Ibid, 2:24). The Prophet was asked to rule in accordance with righteousness and justice. However, after the sad demise of the Prophet, the most important question was that of the legitimacy of the successor of the Prophet. The fundamental question was that of establishing the legitimate rule. It meant as to who had the right to rule in keeping with standard of political justice. In the context of Islām, it has to mean a rule truly expressing the Divine Sovereign Will. The Prophet did not elaborate any procedure of election or selection of his successor, it was for the community of believers to devise any procedure of succession by recourse to consensus. The chosen successor would have to carry out his government in accordance with the standard of justice set in the Qur'ānic Revelations and the Prophetic Traditions. The consensus of the community led to the establishing of the caliphate of Abu Bakr. However, the matter did not end up here. The question of the legitimacy of succession became all the more controversial in coming years.

In course of time, three main interpretations of the principle of legitimacy emerged. Each interpretation representing a political group claims that its principle of legitimacy conformed more accurately with the Qur'ānic Revelations and Prophetic Traditions. In fact, in each interpretation underlined that its principle of legitimacy was the only valid one; only its principle of legitimacy accorded completely with the principle of justice enshrined in the Qur'ān and *Sunnah*.

Sunnītes, Shi'ites and Khwarijites advanced their respective interpretations of the principle of legitimacy and standard of justice. According to Sunnītes, the successor to the Prophet must be a member of Prophet's tribe i.e. from Quraysh. According to Shiites the successor must be of the Prophet's family. The Sunnītes advanced the view that the minimum standard of political justice required that the Divine Sovereign Will must be exercised by a member of the Prophet's tribe. According to Shi'ites the minimum standard of political justice required that the Divine Sovereign Will must be exercised by a member of the Prophet's family. The Shi'ites underlined that only the member of the Prophet's family could exercise the

Divine Sovereign Will with justice. The Sunnītes insisted that membership in the larger circle of the Prophet's tribe was quite adequate for the requirements of political justice. The Shi'ites invoked a tradition that Prophet had already designated Ali to be the first Imām of the Muslims. The Ali, therefore, bequeathed the Imāmate to his descendants in accordance to the rule of seniority. According to the Shi'ite doctrine no other Imām would be qualified or capable of exercising the Sovereign Will with Justice. As against Shi'ites, the Sunnītes rejected the authenticity of this tradition. They advanced another tradition from the Prophet exhorting that the rulers of his community should be from the tribe of the Quraysh. However, the Prophet did not specify as to how any candidate from the tribe should become an Imām or the head of the State. In view of the same, the choice of the Imām rested with the community as a whole.

The Shi'ites emphasised that the first Imām was designated by the Prophet and it was the Prophet who was authorised to exercise God's Sovereign Will. The Prophet imparted to the Imām an esoteric knowledge by recourse to which he was capable of pondering the explicit and implicit meaning of the Revelational Law. Secondly, as a member of the Prophet's family the Imām was blessed with certain qualities by birth and training. These qualities rendered the Imām immune to human limitations. In view of the same, the Imām is deemed to be sinless *(ma 'sum)*, making him capable of not only infallible decision making but of also impeccable character. The membership of the Prophet's house makes Imām the most qualified man to exercise God's Sovereign Will. No person outside the house of the Prophet can ever be deemed capable of exercising God's Will with justice. Thirdly, the Imām is vested with the Charisma inherent in his personality and is uniquely capable of commanding loyalty from his followers. Therefore, he is the only person capable of meeting the challenges and imperatives of political justice. He is only a person qualified to provide requisite leadership and achieve the aims and objectives of the State.

The Sunnītes contested the central contention of Shi'ites that the Prophet had designated Ali as a first Imām. The election or the selection of the Imām has to be carried out by recourse to consensus of the community. They advanced the tradition of the Prophet that the agreement of the community on public affairs is an expression of God's Sovereign Will. The Sunnī theory of Imāmate or Caliphate introduced an element of Popularity into the legitimacy of the Imām. It introduced the consensus of the community as a principle of legitimacy of the Imāmate. The Shī'ah principle of designation tried to obviate the communitarian dimension advanced by the Sunnīs. The Sunnīs underlined that the Prophet had already laid down the principles of religion and *Sharī'ah*. The Imām had to carry out only the implementation of the *Sharī'ah*. The Prophetic legislation had come to an end and now the Imām had to implement the Law and judge among people with justice. The Imām was not necessarily the best of all capable persons to govern. He was certainly not the infallible as stipulated by the Shiite doctrine.

The Shi'ite doctrine of Imāmate underscored that God's Sovereign Will was to be exercised by the Prophet and thereafter by a member of Prophet's family. The arrangement was mandated by the *Sharī'ah* or Law, God authorizing Prophet to exercise His Sovereign Will and Prophet nominating Ali as his successor. The Imāmate would pass on to other members of the Prophet's family. In this arrangement the participation of the community of believers through consensus or consultation was unwarranted and uncalled-for. On the other hand, the Sunnī doctrine of Imāmate or Caliphate introduced an element of democracy in the selection of the Imām or Caliph. The Sunnītes underscored the view that Imām was to be appointed by recourse to consensus of the community and thereafter the Imām had to take decisions and command their implementation by recourse to consultation with scholars and specialists from different walks of life.

Right from the installation of first Caliph Abu Bakr the subsequent control of political power by Umayyads and Abbasids, the Shi'ite questioned the legitimacy of the Sunnīte rule. After the demise of Hazrat Ali in 661, al-Husayn, his second son claimed the Imāmate. However, he was seized by the forces of the Yazid on the outskirts of Karbala near the River Euphrates and put to death along with his relatives and companions in October 680. The descendants of Husayn never gave up their claim to the legitimate Imāmate. They continued their challenge to Sunnī rule till the sudden disappearance of Twelfth Imām in 874. The Shi'ites interpreted the event of disappearance as Imām having gone into *ghayba* (absence) though he is physically absent he is spiritually intimately linked to Shī'ah community of believers. The Twelfth Imām will return at an unspecifiable period of time as al-Mahedi and establish Shī'ah rule in its pristine glory. The hidden Imām will return to establish legitimacy and justice.

There was another school of thought which was radically against both Sunnīte and Shi'ite doctrines of Imāmate or Caliphate known as Kharijites. They advanced a radical notion of political justice. The Kharijites rejected both the Sunnīte and Shi'ite doctrines of legitimacy. They underscored that Sovereignty belongs to God and only God is the legitimate Ruler and Judge of men. The exercise of the power cannot be privilege of a few leaders belonging to established houses and prominent clans. The exercise of power is the responsibility of all men. It is their duty to participate in the administration of social, political and economic affairs in keeping with the scale of justice prescribed in the Qur'ān and the Traditions. All believers are equal in the eyes of Allah and no distinction should be made between them on grounds of caste, class or colour. The only distinction that Qur'ān establishes is that of righteousness. Only righteous people are honourable in the eyes of Allah.

Theoretically speaking, Kharijites held, there was no need of the enforcement of Law by an Imām, if all Muslims did abide by the Law and carry out their duties. However, most of the Kharijites were convinced of the need for an Imām with a view to enforcing Law and achieving justice. An Imām was especially needed for the enforcement of *Sharī'ah*, till Muslims graduated to authentic faithfulness. Imāmate is purely a political institution and any Imām getting corrupt or showing incompetence, could be readily removed from his office. However, Imāmate, under no circumstances can be allowed to be anchored on empty claims of legitimacy advanced by Shi'ites or Sunnītes. The Imāmate could be grounded on some principles of political justice derived from the Qur'ān and the Traditions. Since the Qur'ān or the Traditions do not offer any method of election or selection of an Imām, it was for the community of believers to choose an Imām from among the most highly qualified Muslims irrespective of any consideration of class, colour, race, tribe etc. However, what's more fundamental is to establish a righteous society and educate members of the community into authentic believers. Once such a purpose is achieved, there would be no need for any Imāmate or the State. There would be no logical or doctrinal justification for the State. It shall wither away. In the final analysis, only the rule of Law would prevail (Khadduri, 1984, p. 22). Subsequent to Sunnīte, Shi'ite and Kharijite interpretations of legitimacy and political justice, several schools of thought emerged in course of time. There were Jabarites and Qadarites or Determinists and Free-Willists. The Jabarites held that every action was determined by God and human beings as so called moral agents do not enjoy any moral autonomy or independence. They argued that an overwhelming number of the Qur'ānic verses can be quoted in support of the deterministic stand that man is devoid of any initiative and everything has been predetermined or predestined by God. On the other hand, there were Qadarites who argued that man has been blessed with faculties of understanding as well as will to action and implementation. He is free to do whatever he wants to and can make or unmake his destiny. The Umayyad rules appropriated the Jabarite standpoint and argued that not even a leaf can move without the permission of Allah. He is the master of the power, gives power to whomsoever He wants, snatches power from whomsoever He wants, confers honour on whomsoever He wants and humiliates whomsoever He wants, all that is good is under His control and He has power over all things. The Implication was that everything has decided by God and ascendancy to Caliphate was an outcome of Divine Will. It was in best interest of man to abide by the imperatives of Divine Will and accept it as the ultimate criterion of political justice. The opponents of Umayyads such as Qadarites and Shi'ites underlined the doctrine of human free-will and responsibility. They accused Ummayyads of misinterpreting or misrepresenting and distorting the rear import of the Qur'ānic teachings. It is human beings who as rational and moral agents have to strive for the establishment of a just social, political and economic order.

The Qadarites or Free Willists underlined that all human acts were born out of Divinely granted Will-power to man. Every human being was free to strive for justice or side by the forces of injustice.

> The Qadarites argued that Umayyad Caliphs had by their free will, chosen to exercise God's Sovereignty contrary to the scale of justice laid down in the Law, they had forfeited their right to rule; therefore, their claim to the legitimacy of the Imāmate was null and void (Ibid, 1984, p. 24).

The Umayyads did not accept any of the arguments advanced by Shi'ite or Kharijites with regard to legitimacy. Their fundamental argument was that the Qur'ān and *Sunnah* of the Prophet do not stipulate any clear or categorical rule with regard to selection and election of an Imām, it was clearly the collective duty of community of believers to go in for the selection or election of an Imām by recourse to *Ijma* (consensus). This was the procedure adopted in the election and confirmation of Abu Bakr, Umar, Uthman and Ali. This was the procedure adopted in election and confirmation of Muawiyah as the next Caliph after Ali. The Umayyad rulers also invoked the doctrine of Jabr, holding human acts to be predicted by and not created out of human will. They sought to justify their policies and actions by citing the doctrine of Jabr. The doctrine of Jabr is in accord with the Umayyad position that all the events that had taken place in the past were in accordance with God's Will. The Umayyads sought to identify political justice with the doctrine of predestination. In the process, they sought the support of advocates of Jabr for the Caliphate against their Qadarite opponents.

The deepening controversies with regard to legitimacy and political justice led to wide-spread accusations and counter-accusations of *Kufr* (heresy). The rival political factions declared one another to be apostates. They disqualified one another from the very membership of the community of believers. At this, some conscientious believers were deeply concerned or aroused. They did not approve of religious sanction against believers for their different political opinions. They underlined the need for separating religious and moral questions from political disagreements. They advocated the doctrine of suspension of judgement on political issues of day. They were called Murji'tes. The Murji'tes stressed that rival political leaders or workers must be deemed to be true believers, even when they are accused of heresy by their political rivals; of course, they must be affirming their faith in the unicity of Allah, authenticity of the Prophethood and reality of the Day of Judgement etc. No believers can claim any real knowledge with regard to legitimacy, as to which party was right or wrong. We can know about the truth only on the Day of Judgement when God will pronounce the final word. In view of the same, the Murji'tes underlined the need for suspension of judgement on questions pertaining to different political opinions. The believers, therefore, were under no obligation to take sides on questions of political justice. They are eligible to be Muslims so long as they believe in Allah and the mission of His Apostle (Ibid, pp. 28-29).

Hasan al-Basri (642-728) was one of the leading theologians of the first century of *Hijra*. He was widely reputed for his piety and uprightness. His views on Jabr and Qadr were not categorically spelt out. His stand on Jabr and Qadr seems to have been taken in between lines. He was not of the view that every human act is born out of free-will. He also did not say that all evil and unjust acts were predicated by God as was done by the votaries of Jabr. His views with regard to Qadr were not formulated on rational grounds, as was done by the Qadarites. His views were powerfully oriented by such revelations as follows:

> God does not command indecency; what do you say concerning God such things as you do not know? Say: God command justice (*Al-Qur'ān:* 7: 27-28).

> To any of you that chooses to press forward, or to follow behind; "Every soul will be (held) in pledge for its deeds" (Ibid, 74:37-38).

> On no soul doth Allah place a burden greater than it can bear. It gets every good that it earns, and it suffers every ill that it earns. (Pray:) "Our Lord! Condemn us not if we forget or fall into error; our Lord! Lay not on us a burden like that which Thou didst lay on those before us: Our Lord! Lay not on us a burden greater than we have strength to bear. Blot out our sins, and grant us forgiveness. Have mercy on us. Thou art our Protector; help us against those who stand against Faith." (Ibid, 2:286).

Accordingly, Hasan al-Basri held that God has not created all human acts. He asked man to carry out good deeds in keeping with justice. God also prohibited human beings from undertaking indecent and unjust acts. Hasan al-Basri held that man was dependent on God and yet acts of moral and religious responsibility were born out of human free-will. "Guidance flows from God but wrong doing from man" (Khadduri, 1984, p. 32). Each human being is personally responsible for every act of wrong doing.

Hasan al-Basri made a distinction between political and ethical justice. The ethical justice amounted to righteousness of conduct and commitment to Law and religion. He advanced his views in support of the status quo. However, he justified his support of the established authority by recourse to the Qur'ānic verse: "Obey Allah, and obey the Apostle, and those charged with authority among you" (*Al-Qur'ān:* 4:59). However, he did qualify his standard of political justice by urging the authorities to pursue justice and give up oppression and injustice.

Subsequent to Hasan al-Basri, Mabad al-Juhani and Ghaylan al-Dimashqi emerged as prominent Qadarites and engaged themselves in theological disputes as well as political activities. Both of them were executed by Umayyad authorities for questioning their legitimacy and spreading rebellion across the territory. Their contemporary Jahm B. Safwan, was a radical Jabarite. According to Jahm, everything including human actions was created by God. He argued that the Qadarite perspective on problem of free-will and human responsibility seriously qualifies God's

Omnipotence. According to Jahm, since the world we live in is dominated by God's Will and Absolute power, the question of justice is devoid of any significance or relevance.

On the question of political justice Hasan al-Basri largely remained silent. His views bordered on Murjites and he was prepared to postpone judgement on question of political justice to the hereafter. However, in course of time, his views were subjected to critical scrutiny by some of his leading intellectual disciples. Wasil B. Ata, a disciple of Hasan al-Basri, may specifically be cited as an open critic of Hasan al-Basri's views on political justice. He seceded from his master to form a dissident group and became a forerunner of Mu'tazilite thought. Wasil was a student of Hasan al-Basri. However, in course of time, he developed views and opinions which were neither in accord with Kharijites, nor Murjites and nor with his master Hasan al-Basri. According to Kharijites, a believer who denounces allegiance to the Imām, is an unbeliever; he was supposed to have committed a grave sin. According to Murjites, we should concentrate on our moral and religious duties and responsibilities and suspend our judgement on the question of political justice. Wasil B. Ata took a middle position between Kharijites and Murjites. He worked out his own doctrine known as intermediate position (*al-manzilabayn al-manzilatayen*). He advanced the view that any believing Muslim who denounces allegiance to the Imām can neither be designated to be an unbeliever nor was he to be entirely bereft of infidelity. Such a person was in an intermediate position which is called "*fasiq*". Such a person can be subjected to punishment up to a certain extent. However, he cannot be branded as an unbeliever (Khadduri, 1984, p. 36).

2.5 HUMAN RIGHTS IN ISLĀM

In the history of social, political and economic justice, the emergence of the Qur'ānic world-view and value-system in the first half of seventh century A.D constitutes a turning point. In fact, Islām is anchored on two main planks; its emphasis on *Haquq-Ullah* (rights of God) and *Haquq-a-Ibad* (rights of the servants of Allah). The abstract or revelatory or Qur'ānic term *(Al-Haqq)* signifies both justice and human rights. MajidKhadduri in his book The Islāmic Conception of Justice brings out the following:

> No subject is more closely connected with the concept of justice than "human rights" since justice would be meaningless if the fundamental rights of man were to be unrecognized or ignored by society. In the Revelation, it will be recalled, the two concepts of justice and rights were implied in the abstract term of *"al-haqq,"* which is one of the ultimate goals of the Law. The jurist-theologians, in their discourses on justice, often said that, whereas the object of the Law is justice, its subject matter is the rights and duties of man (Khadduri, 1984, p. 233).

The Qur'ān and the *Sunnah* repeatedly refer to human rights and these rights are accorded to the entire humankind and not to Muslims alone. Islām has granted human rights to all human beings without any discrimination on the grounds of caste, creed or color. Moreover, the human rights in Islām have been granted not by the kings or legislative assemblies but by Allah. In view of the same, these rights cannot be withdrawn by any King or Legislative assembly. No one is entitled to abrogate these rights or withdraw them. Human rights as legal injunctions and moral exhortations have been enshrined in hundreds of the verses of the Qur'ān. In fact, there are two main sources of Human Rights in Islām. Firstly, the Qur'ān is the foremost source of *Sharī'ah* as well as Human Rights. The Qur'ānic provisions are Immutable and constitute the permanent and sacred constitution which cannot be subjected to alternation or suspension. Secondly, Prophet's *Sunnah* is a very important and significant source of Human Rights in Islām. *Sunnah* signifies the verbal pronouncements, practical judgments, implicit approvals, and explicit interpretations, exhortations, interventions, silences and categorical assertions of the Prophet with regard to individual, social, political, economic and legal matters of vital importance. The Qur'ān specifically asks believers to follow Allah, His Prophet and people invested with authority. The traditions of the Prophet constitute a veritable goldmine of justifications and validations with regard to affirmation and implementation of human rights.

Apart from the Qur'ān and *Sunnah* of the Prophet, the appropriation and justification or validation of Human Rights can be carried out by recourse to consensus of Islāmic scholars (*Ijma*) and reasoning of the individual scholars. Muslim scholars can unanimously certify certain rights to be binding and inviolate. Of course, such a unanimous judgment has to be hammered out in the light of the injunctions of the Qur'ān and traditions of the Prophet. The consensus of the scholars with regard to Human Rights or important issues can provide vital inputs in resolving the upcoming and emerging disagreements. However, there is a fourth source of the explication and implementation of Human Rights which is reasoning or *Qiyas*. Apart from consensus, individual scholars can also stipulate and validate Human Rights by recourse to reasoning, *Qiyas* or *Ijtihad*. The individual opinion, judgment or proclamation should also be in accord with the fundamental principles and values enshrined in the Qur'ān and the *Sunnah* of the Prophet. Some of the Human Rights accorded by Islām can be tabulated as hereunder:

RIGHT TO LIFE

It goes without saying that right to life is the most sacred of Human Rights. Islām does not provide us unconditional or unqualified right to life. In Islāmic scale of values, right to life can be sacrificed at the altar of higher values or larger good and welfare of humankind. For example, it is specifically mentioned in the Qur'ān that mischief-mongering is a greater disvalue than the murder of a human being. However, under normal circumstances, Islām provides fully-fledged protection to human life. Islām declares unjustifiable murder of a person to be absolutely unacceptable. The following verse of the Qur'ān brings out the seriousness of the Qur'ānic commitment to the protection of life:

> We ordained for the Children of Israel that if any one slew a person--unless it be for murder or for spreading mischief in the land--it would be as if he slew the whole people: And if any one saved a life, it would be as if he saved the life of the whole people (*Al-Qur'ān*: 5:35).

The following verse of the Qur'ān also brings out the same:

> If a man kills a Believer intentionally, his recompense is Hell, to abide therein (for ever): And the wrath and the curse of Allah are upon him, and a dreadful penalty is prepared for him (Ibid, 4:93).

The Prophet of the Islām declared the sacredness of the Right to Life, "The greatest sins are to associate something with God and to kill a human being" (Mawdudi, 1982, p. 22).

Islām also protects the right to life of an embryo. It also came heavily on the practice of female infanticide carried out by parents during the pre-Islāmic times. The right to life is absolutely sacred, unless such a right is qualified by the grave sins of any person who can be prosecuted under appropriate injunctions promulgated by the Qur'ān. No individual or State can take away one's right to life wantonly. The right to life can be taken away only after appropriate judicial investigation has been carried out according to the commandments or injunctions of Allah as embodied in the Qur'ān.

THE RIGHT TO EQUALITY

Islām lays greatest emphasis on justice and equality. It does not accept the superiority of anyone over anyone else on grounds of language, culture, history, caste, creed, colour or nationality. The following verse of the Qur'ān deserves to be deliberated upon with utmost philosophical or intellectual consideration:

> O mankind! We created you from a single (pair) of a male and a female, and made you into nations and tribes, that ye may know each other (not that ye may despise each other). Verily the most honoured of you in the sight of Allah is (he who is) the most righteous of you. And Allah has full knowledge and is well acquainted (with all things) (*Al-Qur'ān*: 49:13).

The following tradition of the Prophet explicates the above verse of the Qur'ān. The Prophet declared in his speech on *Hujat-ul-Wida* (Fare well Hajj).

> No Arab has any superiority over a non-Arab, nor does a non-Arab have any superiority over an Arab. Nor does a white man has any superiority over a black man, or black man has any superiority on the white man, you are all children of Adam and Adam was created from clay (*Al- Hadīth*, Muslim Sharif, Kitabul-Hajj, p. 70).

Thus, the Qur'ān and the *Sunnah* inculcated great sense of equality and justice among early Muslims. They respected human beings irrespective of caste, creed or colour. In view of the same, they touched human hearts before they intellectually convinced non-Muslims of the truth of Islām. Consequently, Northern and Eastern African tribes were converted to the teachings of Islām. In accordance with the teachings of Islām the Arabs accorded great respect to their African counterparts. The Bilal of Ethiopia was an outstanding companion of the Prophet of Islām. Similarly, the Prophet of Islām appointed his own slave Zaid-bin-Harith as the commander in chief of the Army in Battle of the Muta. A number of contemporary non-Muslim thinkers openly admitted that no other religion has solved the problems of race and colour with same degree of success as Islām did. Apart from racial equality, Islām also oriented Muslims to the realization of social, political, economic cultural, linguistic and gender equality.

RIGHT TO FREEDOM

Man has this inner yearning for freedom. However, he is not and he cannot be completely free, or he is everywhere determined by historical, geographical, socio-political, economic, cultural and intellectual conditions and contingencies. Islām recognizes that man be given social, political, economic, cultural and intellectual freedom. However, Islām also educates free individual believers to qualify their freedom by a scale of do's and don'ts. Islām asks believers to do what is righteous and abstain from what is vicious. Man, according to Islām, is free to do what is *Ma'ruf* (righteous) and abstain from doing what is *Munkar* (unrighteous). Man has been blessed with freedom of will, granted freedom of action and can carry out any action in keeping with his sweat will. However, his freedom of will and action has got to be qualified by a scale of moral values and disvalues. He should not do what is exploitative, oppressive or leads to injustice and enslavement. For example, Islām emerged in early seventh century in Arab society in which institution of slavery was rampantly prevalent. Islām did not specifically ban slavery just as it did ban taking interest on loans or eating pork. It adopted an ameliorative and emancipatory approach towards slavery. The Qur'ān and the traditions of the Prophet encouraged better-off Muslims to liberate slaves by purchasing their freedom. The Qur'ān even allowed the money collected from *Zakat* to be spent on liberating slaves. Thus, Islām created conditions as well as mindset by recourse to which the institution of slavery was fizzled out within around mid-seventh century A.D. However, most importantly, Islām clearly and categorically forbids the primitive practice of capturing free men, making them slaves or settling them into slavery. There is a tradition of the Prophet in which the Prophet of Islām pledges to be a plaintiff on the Day of Judgment against those who enslave a free man, then sell him and eat up the money charged for such an enslavement (Mawdudi, 1982, P. 8). The Prophet of Islām further declared: "He who emancipates a Muslim slave, for every organ of his, Allah will emancipate from Hellfire, an organ of the emancipators" (Ali, 1995, p. 167).

RIGHT TO EXPRESSION

No Islāmic Society or State can snatch any person's right to freely express himself or herself. Each person is entitled to freedom of expression, opinion or interpretation. Each person is free to agree or disagree with any established interpretation or any other emerging alternative point of view. However, Islām does qualify right to expression as it does qualify right to freedom. Under normal circumstances, Islām does accord right to freedom of thought and expression to every member of the society. The citizens of the Islāmic State are free to express different opinions with regard to various issues. However, the freedom of expression must be instrumental to propagation of virtue and truth. It should not be used to express evil or wickedness (Hussain, 1991, p. 24). The freedom of expression has to be oriented to bidding what's proper and forbidding what's improper (*Al-Qur'ān:* 22:41). Those who believe in Allah have to command what's proper and forbid what's improper (Ibid, 3:110). Freedom of speech and expression cannot be used for spreading blasphemy and ill-will. The Prophet of Islām used to passionately listen to all that was expressed in his court. So did his rightly-guided Caliphs. The Prophet of Islām never imposed his views especially with regard to worldly matters on his companions. The Prophet declared: "when I advise you in respect of any worldly matters don't forget that I am a human being" (Mahmood, 1993, pp. 41-42).

Islām accords the right to protest against tyranny and injustice, to all human beings. The citizens of an Islāmic State can protest against the State, against the ruler of the State or any highly placed individual in the Society or State. The Prophet of Islām declared: "One who protests against a tyrant is the greatest crusader" (Ibid, p. 43). The Prophet further declared: "The people who endorse the wrong doings of the rulers after me are not my followers" (*Al-Hadīth*, Muslim Sharief, Kitab-ul-Hajj). The right to *Ijtihad* or personal interpretation is also indicative of freedom of expression in Islāmic philosophy and jurisprudence.

RIGHT TO FREEDOM OF CONSCIENCE

Islām accords all human beings the right to freedom of conscience. Non-Muslims can be motivated to accept Islām. However, no Muslim can compel them to accept Islām. No Muslim has the authority to enforce his religion on non-Muslims. The following verse of the Qur'ān illustrates the same:

> Let there be no compulsion in religion: Truth stands out clear from Error: Whoever rejects Evil and believes in Allah hath grasped the most trustworthy handhold, that never breaks. And Allah heareth and knoweth all things (*Al-Qur'ān*: 2:256).

Another verse of the Qur'ān takes a more categorical and radical view of the right to freedom of conscience accorded by Islām to all human beings: "To you be your Way, and to me mine" (Ibid, 109:6).

It is utterly unacceptable to Islām to compel non-Muslims to get converted to Islām. Anyone can accept Islām by his own choice. Once a person is converted to Islām out of his own choice, the Muslims will have to welcome him and accord him all the rights and privileges that other members of the community are entitled to. Those who are not converted to Islām out of their own choice, have every right to stay put wherever they are. Their refusal not to accept Islām or their decision not to get converted to Islām, will have to be respected. No moral, social or political pressure can be put on such a person with a view to changing his mind. No Islāmic society or government can stop non-Muslims from propagating their religion. Non-Muslims are also entitled to construct their places of worship and preserve their other marks of identity. Islām accords full freedom to non-Muslims to observe their respective religions. Non-Muslims enjoy social, educational and cultural rights to the fullest possible extent.

RIGHT TO JUSTICE

The Qur'ān has laid greatest emphasis on right to justice in scores of its verses. The following verses of the Qur'ān bring out the unqualified emphasis:

> O ye who believe! Violate not the sanctity of the Symbols of Allah, nor of the Sacred Month, nor of the animals brought for sacrifice, nor the garlands that mark out such animals, nor the people resorting to the Sacred House, seeking of the bounty and good pleasure of their Lord. But when ye are clear of the Sacred Precincts and of pilgrim garb, ye may hunt and let not the hatred of some people in (once) shutting you out of the Sacred Mosque lead you to transgression (and hostility on your part). Help ye one another in righteousness and piety, but help ye not one another in sin and rancor: Fear Allah: For Allah is strict in punishment (Ibid, 5:3).

> And call in remembrance the favor of Allah unto you, and his Covenant, which he ratified with you, when ye said: "We hear and we obey": And fear Allah, for Allah knoweth well the secrets of your hearts (Ibid, 5:8).

> O ye who believe! Stand out firmly for justice, as witnesses to Allah, even as against yourselves, or your parents, or your kin, and whether it be (against) rich or poor: For Allah can best protect both. Follow not the lusts (of your hearts), lest ye swerve, and if ye distort (justice) or decline

to do justice, verily Allah is well acquainted with all that ye do (Ibid, 4:135).

The followers of Islām are asked to be just towards all human beings. Justice goes beyond tribes, nations, races, or communities. All human beings across the globe are entitled to justice. Muslims cannot afford to be unjust towards any human being in the world (Mawdudi, 1969, p. 29).

RIGHT TO PROPERTY

Islām confers the right of security of ownership of property to all the lawful holders of property. No one is allowed to take possession of a property unless it is acquired by lawful means. The Qur'ān categorically declares: "Don't devour one another's wealth by false and illegal means" (*Al-Qur'ān*: 2:188).

RIGHT TO EDUCATION

Islām laid greatest emphasis on education, learning, knowledge, reasoning and research. The first verse of the Qur'ān declares:

> Iqraa, or Read! or Proclaim! orAlaq, or The Clot of Congealed Blood. In the name of Allah, Most Gracious, Most Merciful. Proclaim! (or Read!) in the name of thy Lord and Cherisher, Who created (Ibid, 96:1).
>
> Created man, out of a (mere) clot of congealed blood (Ibid, 96:2).Taught man that which he knew not (Ibid, 96:5).

Islām laid highest emphasis on graduating from darkness to light. The Qur'ān underscores that only man of understanding can appreciate Allah's signs and verses of the Qur'ān. The Prophet of Islām said, "Of all that the father can give his children and the best is their good education and training" (*Al-Hadīth* Miskhat, KitabulIlm). The Prophet also asked some prisoners of war from Battle of Badr to teach some Muslim children how to read and write (Al-Minwai, 1993, p. 49). The Prophet is also reported to have said: "seeking knowledge is sacred duty; it is obligatory on every Muslim, male and female" (Ibid, p. 52).

Thus, Islām makes education to be obligatory on Muslims. Seeking knowledge is mandatory rather than recommendatory. In an Islāmic Society or State Muslims and non-Muslim both can be enforced to go in for appropriate educational and training programmes.

RIGHT TO PROTECTION OF HONOUR

Islām prescribes that all human beings are entitled to honour and prestige. There is a clear-cut Qur'ānic injunction that asks believers to be deferential towards other human beings even when they have limitations and shortcomings. The Qur'ān declares:

> O ye who believe! Let not some men among you laugh at others: It may be that the (latter) are better than the (former): Nor let some women laugh at others: It may be that the (latter) are better than the (former): Nor defame nor be sarcastic to each other, nor call each other by (offensive) nicknames: Ill-seeming is a name connoting wickedness, (to be used of one) after he has believed: And those who do not desist are (indeed) doing wrong (*Al-Qur'ān*: 49:11).

> O ye who believe! Avoid suspicion as much (as possible): For suspicion in some cases is a sin: And spy not on each other, nor speak ill of each other behind their backs. Would any of you like to eat the flesh of his dead brother? Nay, ye would abhor it. ..But fear Allah: For Allah is Oft-Returning, Most Merciful (Ibid, 49:12).

The above verses of the Qur'ān clearly prohibit the practice of insulting one another, defamation, backbiting, libel and sarcasm. The Prophet of Islām prohibited speaking ill of other persons in their absence. It is *ghibat* if we speak ill of others in their absence. However, it is *ghibat* only if what we speak about others is true and such behaviour is clearly prohibited. However, if we say something about in their absence which is not true, it is slander or calumny (*Bhutan*) and such behaviour is all the more a worse crime. So Islām prohibits both mud-slinging and slandering. Even when some people have personality limitations and short-comings, others have no business to talk about them in their absence (Mahmood, 1993, p. 43).

RIGHT TO PRIVACY

Islām respects the right of privacy of every human being. The following verses of the Qur'ān clearly bring out the recognition of the right to privacy by Islām:

> O ye who believe! Enter not houses other than your own, until ye have asked permission and saluted those in them: That is best for you, in order that ye may heed (what is seemly) (*Al-Qur'ān*: 24:27).

> If ye find no one in the house, enter not until permission is given to you: If ye are asked to go back, go back: That makes for greater purity for yourselves: And Allah knows well all that ye do (Ibid, 24:28).

The Prophet of Islām prescribed:

> That a man peeping unlawfully into another person's house could be lawfully rendered blind. Also he specifically asked his people not to poke their nose into others personal affairs, not to bug confidential conversations between others, and not to glance through what was being written for or by others (Mahmood, 1993, p. 44).

Thus, Islām asks people not only to be legally correct but also to be decent and morally correct.

RIGHT TO PROTEST AGAINST TYRANNY

The right to protest against tyranny is a recognized right in Islām. The best form of *Jihad* (Holy war), according to the Prophet of Islām, is protesting against a tyrant ruler (*Al-Hadīth*, Nisaai, Vol. VII, p. 161). Another Tradition of the Prophet says:

> Whosoever see's evil with his eyes should stop it with his hands, if this is not possible then with the word of mouth, and if even this is not possible (at least) hate it heartily; and this is the weakest state of faith (Mawdudi, 1982, p. 42).

The above tradition of the Prophet clearly brings out the anti-establishmentarian character of Islām. If individuals or groups of people somehow manage to usurp power and tyrannize people, then Muslims have every right to protest against such a rule and fight against the powers that be to their fullest possible extent. Islām has categorically granted the right to protest against tyranny and no one upon the Earth has the authority to deny such a right to Muslims (Shamsi, 2003, p. 198).

RIGHT TO FREEDOM OF ASSOCIATION

Islām provides Muslims the right to freedom of association. They can form organizations or parties. The following verse of the Qur'ān is pertinent in this regard: "Let there arise out of you a band of people inviting to all that is good, enjoining what is right, and forbidding what is wrong: They are the ones to attain felicity" (*Al-Qur'ān*: 3:104). The above verse signifies that people are free to organize or associate with a view to promoting what's virtuous and controlling what's vicious. Muslims should organize themselves to propagate virtue and righteousness. They should never organize with a view to spreading what's evil. During the Caliphate of Hazrat Ali the Khaijities openly abused Hazrat Ali and threatened to kill him. Hazrat Ali never arrested them for such offences. He told his officers that mere abusive language or threats were not enough to arrest our opponents; unless, of course, they actually do any crime, they cannot be arrested. Thus, Hazrat Ali gave unparalleled freedom to opposition. Even those who threatened him with murder were not arrested by him (Hussain, 1991, p. 35).

RIGHTS OF ENEMIES OF WAR

Islām has enacted rules with regard to conduct of war as and when it happens. These rules bring out the humane face of Islāmic principles. Muslims have been asked not to conduct hostilities against their enemies unless a war has been declared against them formally. Or unless the enemies have on their own initiated aggression against them. Muslims have been forbidden from attacking wounded soldiers or those soldiers who are not fit to fight. The Prophet of Islām asked Muslims not to put any prisoner to sword, not to kill anyone who is tied or is in captivity, not to burn alive, not to indulge in pillage or plunder, not to destroy residential areas (Mawdudi, 1982, p. 55).

Islām has categorically prohibited believers for taking anything from the general public of conquered country. Muslims have been asked not to disgrace or mutilate the corpses of their enemies as was done before the advent of Islām.

SAFEGUARDS AGAINST VIOLATION

Besides providing human rights, Islām also provides certain theological or ideological safeguards with a view to protecting human rights. The first and foremost Islāmic belief is that Allah alone is the Creator, Sustainer and Master of the universe. Only Allah has the right to command us to do something or forbid us from doing something else. Allah alone vests the Sovereignty and He has the right or authority to prescribe anything or proscribe anything. Faith in the Ultimate Sovereignty of Allah cuts at the very roots of enslavement of Man by man or lordship of man over man. Thus, faith in the Sovereignty of Allah serves as the first safeguard against the violation of Human rights. It erodes the very ideology of rule of man over man culminating into widespread violation of human rights across history (Hussain, 1991, p. 55).

Secondly, every man is deemed and defined to be vicegerent of Allah upon this Earth. They cannot do anything substantial on their own, they have to do as they are directed to do. They have to perform all their activities in keeping with the instructions and injunctions prescribed in the Qur'ān. They cannot change, amend or restrict any of the rights granted by Allah. Man is a trustee and whatever powers he is given, have got be exercised according to the injunctions advanced by Allah. Every trustee of some power or office is accountable to people in this world and to Allah in the hereafter. Thus, vicegerency and trusteeship of man along with Sovereignty of Allah are three important safeguards against the violation of human rights in Islām.

UNIVERSAL ISLĀMIC DECLARATION OF HUMAN RIGHTS

The Universal Islāmic Declaration of Human Rights is a document created by Islāmic Councils in Paris and London. It restates basic human rights using the language of Islāmic jurisprudence. The difference between the original Arabic version and the official English translation has been described as "very Problematic." Among other problems, Mayer notes that throughout the document, references specifically to *Sharī'ah* law are mentioned only as "the Law," which could mislead readers of only the English version.

Similar documents include the "Draft Charter on Human and People's Right in the Arab world", endorsed by the Arab Union of Lawyers in 1987, and the "Cairo Declaration on Human Rights in Islām", adopted by the Organisation of Islāmic Conference in 1990.

The rise of Modern West after sixteenth century Renaissance and Reformation, has signified a turning point in the World of history in all its implications; social, political, economic, cultural, intellectual, philosophical etc. The replacement of Tolemic astronomy by Copernican astronomy or of geocentric hypothesis by heliocentric hypothesis in sixteenth century was really an astounding and outstanding breakthrough in the annals of human thought. It changed the entire climate of thought in Europe and subsequently outside Europe as well. The rise of modern philosophy through Descartes, Spinoza, Locke, Leibnitz etc coincided with Bacon's philosophy of science and astrophysics of Galileo and Newton. The emergence, installation and consolidation of heliocentric astronomy in seventeenth century provided a new or radical perspective of understanding and interpretation. Subsequent to extraordinary and significant philosophical and intellectual developments in seventeenth century Europe, the eighteenth century was a full-fledged turnaround. This century was designated as Age of Reason or Age of Enlightenment. The new European world-view and value-system were presided over by scientific and technological standards of investigation, interpretation, evaluation and interrogation. The classical Christian world-view and value-system were given an almost complete send-off and principles of science were given a presiding role in the cultural and intellectual areas of operation. It was under Enlightenment beliefs and values that new scientific developments, social scientific investigations, philosophical interpretations and ideological systematizations were proliferated during eighteenth and nineteenth centuries in Europe. New ideologies such as liberalism, Capitalism, socialism, Democracy, Secularism, Pluralism etc were articulated by such European thinkers as Locke, Voltaire, Rousseau, Adam Smith, J.S. Mill, Karl Marx and many more. All these ideologies were humanistic and secular. They aimed at providing justice, freedom, human rights and welfare to all members of the society without any regard to caste, creed, colour, language, culture, history etc.

After the end of world war second in 1945, the United Nations Organization was formed. Apart from many other things the United Nations Organisation also passed Universal Declaration of Human Rights in 1948. The main highlights of this Declaration are as follows:

1. Right to Equality.
2. Freedom from Discrimination.
3. Right to Life, Liberty, Personal Security.
4. Freedom from Slavery.
5. Freedom from Torture and Degrading Treatment.
6. Right to Recognition as a person before the Law.
7. Right to Equality before the Law.
8. Right to Remedy by Competent Tribunal.
9. Freedom from Arbitrary Arrest and Exile.
10. Right to Fair Public Hearing.
11. Right to be Considered Innocent until Proven Guilty.
12. Freedom from Interference with Privacy, Family, Home and Correspondence.
13. Right to Free Movement in and out of the Country.
14. Right to Asylum in other Countries from persecution.
15. Right to a Nationality and the Freedom to Change it.
16. Right to Marriage and Family.

17. Right to Own Property.
18. Freedom of Belief and Religion.
19. Freedom of Opinion and information.
20. Right of Peaceful Assembly and Association.
21. Right to Participate in Government and in Free Elections.
22. Right to Social Security.
23. Right to Desirable Work to Join Trade Unions.
24. Right to Rest and Leisure.
25. Right to Adequate Living Standard.
26. Right to Education.
27. Right to Participate in the Cultural Life of Community.
28. Community Duties Essential to Free and Full Development.
29. Right to a Social Order that Articulates this Document.
30. Freedom from State or Personal Interference in the above Rights.

By and large or broadly speaking Islām is the forerunner and the real champion of the Rights. It bestowed upon the man the human rights when the entire world was under the religio-political tyranny. The United Nation's charter is a very feeble copy of the rights which the Islām had to humanity. Islām has championed human rights since its very inception in early seventh century A.D. In fact, Islām may be said to be a Human Rights Movement since its very beginning. In the light of human rights enshrined in UNO's Declaration of Human Rights, Muslim scholars and intellectuals across the globe authored in 1981 another Declaration of Human Rights within the framework of Islāmic beliefs and values. The main features of this Declaration may be summarily brought out as hereunder:

The first article of the Declaration underlines that life is sacred and inviolate and deserves protection at all cost. No one should be injured or sentenced to death except under the due process of Law. Even after someone is dead, his or her dead body too is inviolate and a dead body deserves to be handled with due solemnity (Universal Islāmic Declaration of Human Rights, Right to Life, Dhul Qaidah 1401, 1981, Article I).

In its article second, it is declared that human freedom too is inviolate and no one's freedom can be violated except under due process of Law. Every human person has inalienable, physical, cultural, economic and political freedom. Every human being is entitled to struggle against any abrogation of his freedom and each oppressed individual or people can legitimately seek the support of other peoples or individuals while carrying out any such struggle (Universal Islāmic Declaration of Human Rights, Right to Freedom, Article II).

The Article third of the Declaration underlines that all persons are equal before Law. They are entitled to equal opportunities, equal wages for equal work and no person can be denied the opportunity to work or be discriminated against on grounds of religion, colour, race, sex, language etc (Universal Islāmic Declaration of Human Rights, Right to Equality and Prohibition against impermissible Discrimination, Article III).

Fourthly, every person is entitled to justice. Everyone has both the right and the duty to protest against injustice, to seek legal remedy against any unwarranted personal injuries or loss. Each human person has a right to defend himself against any charges and to seek fair adjudication by recourse to an independent judicial process. Besides, every person has the right to safeguard the rights of other individuals or communities. No person shall be discriminated in any manner, for championing any rights of individuals and communities. Every Muslim has right to refuse, to obey any command which is against Law (Universal Islāmic Declaration of Human Rights, Right to justice, Article IV).

Fifthly, every person has a right to fair treatment. It is not fair to punish any person before he or she is adjudged guilty of an offence by an independent judicial process. Everybody is entitled to reasonable opportunity for defence. The award of punishment has to be in keeping with the Law, in accordance to the seriousness of the crime and after due consideration of the conditions under which the crime was committed. Any act has got to be stipulated as a crime in a duly declared Statutory Book. Each individual is responsible for his or her actions and there cannot be any vicarious extension of responsibility to other members of the family who have not directly or indirectly participated in the commission of the crime (Universal Islāmic Declaration of Human Rights, Right to Fair Trial, Article V).

Sixthly, every person has the Right to Protection against Abuse of Power. The official agencies have no right to unnecessarily harass any person. Every person has a right to self-defence to the charges made against him. A person can be charged only if a suspicion of his involvement in crime can be reasonably raised. (Universal Islāmic Declaration of Human Rights, Right to Protection Against Abuse of Power, Article VI).

Seventhly, every person has the Right to Protection against torture. No person can be subjected to physical and mental torture. No person can be threatened with injury or forced to do something which is injurious to his interests (Universal Islāmic Declaration of Human Rights, Right to Protection Against Torture, Article VII).

Eighthly, every human being has the right to the protection of his honour. Each human being has the right to protect his reputation. Each person can defend against calumnies. Each person has the right to respond to groundless charges made against him. Each person can defend his honour and fame against any blackmail (Universal Islāmic Declaration of Human Rights, Right to Protection of Honour and Reputation, Article VIII).

Ninthly, all persecuted or oppressed people have the right to seek refuge and asylum. Every person has got this right without any consideration of his race, religion, colour and sex. The Sacred house of Allah known as al-Masjid-al Haram at Mekkah is a declared sanctuary for all Muslims (Universal Islāmic Declaration of Human Rights, Right to Asylum, Article IX).

Tenthly, the religious minorities will enjoy equal rights with their Muslim counterparts to perform their religious duties as per their prescriptions and stipulations. The non-Muslim minorities can have the choice either to be governed in their civil and personal matters by Islāmic Law or by their own personal Laws. The religious rights of non-Muslims will be governed in the light of the *Qurān*ic principle "there is no compulsion in religion" (Universal Islāmic Declaration of Human Rights, Rights of Minorities, Article X).

Eleventhly, every person will have the right and obligation to participate in the Conduct and Management of Public Affairs. Any individual believer of the community is entitled to aspire for and to assume any public office. The government and the people are bound to each other by the process of free consultation (*Shura*). It is through the process of free consultation that people can choose their rulers and it is again through the process of free consultation that the rulers can be removed by the people (Universal Islāmic Declaration of Human Rights, Right and Obligation of Participation in the Conduct and Management of Public Affairs, Article XI).

Twelfthly, every person has the right to Freedom of Belief, Thought and Speech. Any person in an Islāmic State has the right to bring out his thoughts and beliefs. However, any expression of thoughts and beliefs has to be within the limits prescribed by the Law. No person has the right to disseminate falsehood. No person has the right to report anything which leads to indecency or to slander or defames other people. However, every Muslim has not only the right but a duty to pursue knowledge and search for truth. Every Muslim has the right to protest against oppression (Universal Islāmic Declaration of Human Rights, Right to Freedom of Belief, Thought and Speech, Article XII).

Thrirteenthly, every person will enjoy the right to Freedom of Religion. It is obligatory on all Muslims to respect the religious feelings of non-Muslims. No Muslims have the right to hold in contempt or ridicule the religious tenets of non-Muslims. No Muslim can incite public hostility against non-Muslim minorities. All persons across the globe have the right to freedom of conscience. All are entitled to worship in keeping with their beliefs (Universal Islāmic Declaration of Human Rights, Right to Freedom of Religion, Article XIII).

Fourteenthly, every human person has the right to Free Association. Any human being can both individually and collectively participate in the Political, cultural, social and religious life of their community. They are free to establish institutions and agencies, exhorting people to do what's righteous and forbidding them from what's unrighteous. All human beings, both at the individual and collective planes, have a right to create conditions by recourse to which the members of the community can strive for the fullest possible development of their personalities (Universal Islāmic Declaration of Human Rights, Right to Free Association, Article XIV).

Fifteenthly, every person is entitled equal economic benefits from natural resources. The economic resources are the blessings bestowed by Allah on all human beings. Every human person is entitled to pursue his economic interests according to the Law. Every human being can own any property as an individual or in association with others. Some economic resources can be owned by the State in the interest of public welfare. The poor are entitled to certain share in the wealth of rich as prescribed by the Qur'ān. The natural resources need to be harnessed to promote the welfare of the community. Islām forbids certain monopolies, unreasonable trade practices, usury, use of coercion and misleading advertisements with a view to developing balanced economy free of exploitation. Any economic activity can be carried out in an Islāmic society unless it is against the interest of the community or violation of Islāmic Laws and values (Universal Islāmic Declaration of Human Rights, The Economic Order and the Rights Evolving Therefrom, Article XV).

Sixteenthly, every human being is entitled to protection of his property. No person can be expropriated unless it is compelled by the imperative of public interest. However, any expropriation can be worked out on payment of fair and adequate compensation (Universal Islāmic Declaration of Human Rights, Right to protection of Property, Article XVI).

Seventeenthly, every worker in an Islāmic society is entitled to a basic status and dignity. Islām asks Muslims to respect workers and not only to treat them justly but also generously. Every worker is to be paid his wages promptly and every worker is entitled to adequate rest and leisure (Universal Islāmic Declaration of Human Rights, Status and Dignity of Workers, Article XVII).

Eighteenthly, every person has a right to Social Security. Every member of the society is entitled to food, shelter, clothing, education and medicare in accordance with the resources of the society. It is specially the right of those people who cannot take care of themselves out of some disability (Universal Islāmic Declaration of Human Rights, Right to Social Security, Article XVIII).

Nineteenthly, all members of the society have right to enter into marital bound and found a family. The parents have a right to bring up their children in accordance with their religious and cultural traditions. The parents have their rights and privileges and have also to carry out their obligations as stipulated by the Law. Each spouse has the right to be treated with respect and consideration from the other spouse. The wife and children are entitled to be maintained according to the means of the head of the family. The children are entitled to be maintained and properly brought up by their parents. The child labour leading to the underdevelopment of children has got to be legally forbidden. In case parents are unable to properly bring up their children, it is the responsibility of the community to look after them at public expense. Each member of the community has the right to financial support, care and protection from his family, be he a child and an elderly fellow or an incapacitated person. Elderly parents have the right to be financially supported, taken care of and protected by their children. Every mother has the right to respect, care and support from her children. The members of the family have the responsibility to utilize their natural endowments, talents and capabilities for the welfare of their children and other relatives. Nobody has the authority to get any man or woman married against his or her will. No person can suffer diminution of legal personality on account of a marital relationship with person of his or her choice (Universal Islāmic Declaration of Human Rights, Right to Found a Family and Related matters, Article XIX).

Twentiethly, married women have their own rights and privileges. Every married woman has a right to live in the house in which her husband resides. Every married woman is entitled to receive financial or material support in order to maintain a reasonable standard of living. In case she is divorced, she has the right to receive means of maintenance during statutory period of waiting. Every woman has a right to seek and obtain dissolution of marriage as per terms of Law. Besides, women are entitled to inherit from her husband, her parents, her children and other relatives according to the Law (Universal Islāmic Declaration of Human Rights, Rights of Married Women, Article XX). Furthermore, every person is entitled to education and choice of profession. Each person has right to develop his or her personality, move in and outside of his or her country according to Law and no person can be forced to move in or outside any country without negotiating the relevant rules and Laws.

THE CAIRO DECLARATION OF HUMAN RIGHTS IN ISLĀM (1990)

The Member States of the Organisation of Islāmic Conference worked out a Declaration of Human Rights in Islām at Cairo in 1990, known as Cairo Declaration of Human Rights in Islām (CDHRI). This Declaration advances an overview on the Islāmic perspective on Human Rights. The Islāmic *Sharī'ah* is affirmed to be the sole source of such a Declaration of Human Rights. The Declaration supposedly qualifies the Universal Declaration of Human Rights (UDHR) passed by United Nation in

1948). Muslim countries were generally critical of UDHR for ignoring the cultural and religion context of non-Western countries. They deemed UDHR to be a secular understanding of Judeo-Christian tradition, whose implementation can violate the prescribed limits of revealed Law of Islām. In view of the same, the Cairo Declaration of Human Rights in Islām was adopted on August 5, 1990 by forty five foreign ministers of the Organisation of the Islāmic Conference. The Declaration was meant to serve as guidance in matters pertaining to human rights in the social, political, economic, legal and cultural spheres of operation across Muslims States.

At the very outset the Declaration forbids "any discrimination on the base of race, colour, language, belief, sex, religion, political affiliation, social status and or other considerations" (Cairo Declaration on Human Rights in Islām, Aug. 5, 1990, U.N. GAOR)The CDHRI, affirms the sanctity of life and accepts preservation of human life as a duty prescribed by the *Sharī'ah*. The Declaration grants, "Non-belligerents such as old men, women, and children, wounded and sick, and prisoners of war, the right to food, shelter, safety and Medicare in time so far" (De Preux, J. 1994). The Declaration affirmed acts of terrorism to be a violation of human rights. The Declaration grants men and women the right to get married without any regard to race, colour or nationality. However, it affirmed religion to be an important consideration in this regard. The Declaration grants women equal human dignity, right to enjoy and duties to perform. They have been granted financial independence and the right to retain their name and lineage. According to CDHRI the husband is responsible for the social and financial protection of the family. Both parents are granted the rights over their children and make it obligatory upon both of them to protect the child both at pre-natal and post-natal levels. The Declaration grants every family the right to privacy. Besides, no family can be evicted from their residence nor can their property be demolished or confiscated. The Declaration in its Article X states "Islām is the religion of unspoiled nature. It is prohibited to exercise any form of compulsion on man or to exploit his poverty or ignorance in order to convert him to another religion or to atheism" (Lawson, 1995, p. 177). It is forbidden to convert anyone from Islām to another religion or to atheism. The CDHRI, furthermore, protects every person from arbitrary arrest, torture, maltreatment and indignity. The Declaration stipulates that no individual can be used for scientific or medical experimentation. No person can be taken as a hostage for any purpose whatsoever.

Furthermore, according to CDHRI every accused person is to be presumed innocent till he is proven otherwise. Every defendant has got to be given every facility to prove him innocent. The Article XIX of the Declaration brings out that only Islāmic *Sharī'ah* can be the source or authority to define which of actions is a crime and what kind of punishment should be given to any proven criminal. The *Sharī'ah* provides such corporal punishments as whippings, imputations and capital punishment. It is held by the CDHRI that the right to hold public office can be exercised in keeping with the provisions of *Sharī'ah*, which exhorts Muslims not to surrender to non-Muslim rule. It is underscored by the Declaration that every person is fully entitled to freedom and self determination and no individual or community can be enslaved, oppressed, exploited and colonised. The CDHRI commits itself to the rule of Law and establishment of equality and justice. Each person according to Declaration, is entitled to participate in the administration of public affairs of one's country. While the principles of *Sharī'ah* are inviolate, anybody is free to express his opinions freely. Only such opinions must not be contrary to the *Sharī'ah*. Each person has the right to propagate what's right and advocate what's good. Each person has the right to stop what's wrong and evil in the light of the norms of *Sharī'ah*. No person has the right to exploit the right to freedom of expression by violating the sanctity and dignity of the Prophets or undermine moral values and articles of Islāmic faith. Nobody has any right to arouse nationalistic or doctrinal hatred or incite racial discrimination. All the rights and freedoms are subject to the Islāmic *Sharī'ah*. The entire *Ummah* has the responsibility to defend the principles of *Sharī'ah* and true faith.

The fundamental human rights enshrined in the Qur'ān are granted by Allah. They do not originate from manmade Laws. They are Divine in nature and origin and therefore have universal application. The purpose of such freedom or rights is enrichment, humanity, beauty, goodness, success and prosperity of human beings. All human beings across the globe are entitled to these freedoms and rights. Human rights discourse did not begin with UDHR of 1948. Human rights were promulgated 1400 years ago in the Qur'ān and *Sunnah*. Islām advanced an international charter of human rights. It guaranteed some fundamental rights which have been incorporated in the international Laws of our times (Patwari, P. 49).

2.6 WOMEN'S STATUS IN ISLĀM

All human beings ought to be having equal human rights. It so appears to us and is not actually happening to be the case. Human beings do not actually enjoy equal human rights. Historically speaking, there have been discriminations on grounds of race, colour, language, nationality, religion, gender, caste, creed, class etc. There has been wide-spread discrimination, exploitation and tyranny on these and various other such grounds. Women have been denied human rights in almost all civilizations and cultural traditions. As a gender, they have been accorded a second class status. Among all religious traditions, Islām is the first religious tradition, world-view and value-system which has accorded same rights to all human beings without any discrimination on the grounds of gender.

Islām accords women right to inheritance. Throughout history, women have been denied property rights. Such a denial of property rights makes her powerless, weak and indecisive. Furthermore, the denial of property or inheritance rights makes woman completely dependent on their husbands, sons and other relatives. With a view to squaring out this anomaly, the Qur'ān prescribes: "From what is left by parents and those nearest related there is a share for men and a share for women, whether the property be small or large, --a determinate share" (*Al-Qur'ān*: 4:7).

The above verse provides a rule for inheritance for both men and women. Women like men, have a determined share in the property of their parents as well as in the property of their husbands and sons. This verse must be supplemented by the following verse which fixes share in the property of a deceased person:

> Allah (thus) directs you as regards your children's (inheritance): To the male, a portion equal to that of two females: If only daughters, two or more, their share is two thirds of the inheritance; if only one, her share is a half. For parents, a sixth share of the inheritance to each, if the deceased left children; if no children, and the parents are the (only) heirs, the mother has a third; if the deceased left brothers (or sisters) the mother has a sixth. (The distribution in all cases is) after the payment of legacies and debts. Ye know not whether your parents or your children are nearest to you in benefit. These are settled portions ordained by Allah; and Allah is All-Knowing, All-Wise (Ibid, 4:11).

The shares of property as prescribed in the above verse of the Qur'ān can be classified as follows:

1. (a) The first and foremost share holder of the deceased property is his children which includes both boys and girls. So, regarding inheritance not only the sons have the exclusive right to it but also the daughters have their share in it. The sons inherit twice the share of the daughter. Suppose, the deceased has a boy and a girl, the property left by him shall be divided into three equal portions, one third of the portions goes to the daughter and two third of that goes to the son.

(b) Again if there are two daughters and one son, then the property shall be divided into four equal parts, two fourth of the portions or half of the property goes to the two daughters or to each one fourth and the remaining half or the twice of the daughters goes to the son.

(c) Another situation, mentioned in the above verse, is that if there are no sons but more than two daughters then the daughters shall get two third of the property, meaning thereby, the whole property will be divided into three parts and two parts of that will be equally divided between them. If there are three daughters, that two parts (2/3) will be divided into three equal portions and if there are four daughters, that two parts (2/3) will be divided into four equal portions. Here the issue of more than two daughters is mentioned, but if there are two daughters then also their portion remains the same, i.e.- two thirds, (one third to each).

(d) If there is no son but only one daughter, then she will inherit the half of the total property and the rest being divided among other relatives. This leads us to the point that if there is only one boy then he must get the whole property since his share is twice that of the daughter.

2. After the children the parents have the priority in the matter of rights to inherit the property of the deceased. In the absence of the children only the parents inherit the property of the deceased, the father and the mother will inherit one third of that. But if the deceased has no children but has brothers and sisters then the mother will get one sixth of the property and if the deceased has children then also her portion remains same (Begum, 2015, pp. 132-133).

Besides, regarding the shares of husband and wife in inheritance it is declared in the Qur'ān in the following way:

In what your wives leave, your share is a half, if they leave no child; but if they leave a child, ye get a fourth; after payment of legacies and debts. In what ye leave, their share is a fourth, if ye leave no child; but if ye leave a child, they get an eighth; after payment of legacies and debts. If the man or woman whose inheritance is in question, has left neither ascendants nor descendants, but has left a brother or a sister, each one of the two gets a sixth; but if more than two, they share in a third; after payment of legacies and debts; so that no loss is caused (to any one). Thus is it ordained by Allah; and Allah is All-Knowing, Most Forbearing (*Al-Qur'ān:* 4:12).

The above mentioned verse brought out the following principles of property with regard to the share of husband and wife, brothers and sisters:

1. The husband gets half of the inheritance of his wife's property if she has no children. But if she has children then the husband will get one fourth of the wife's property. On the other hand, the wife gets one eight of the husband's property if there are children and one fourth of the same if there are no children.

2. The children, parents, husband and wife are the inheritors in every case. It is worth mentioning here that "in matters of inheritance Abu Bakr, the first Caliph of Islām, used '*qiyas*' (analogical deduction). The Qur'ān prescribes the share of the father. But Abu Bakr by using *qiyas* extended this right to the father's father also (grand-father) (khan, 1999, p. 53). In the above verse ascendants involves grand father and grandmother along with the parents of the deceased. Again, there is '*ijma'* (consensus or collective opinion of jurists) on it that progeny or descendants involve grandsons and grand-daughters also along with the children of the deceased. Hence, grand-father and mother, grand-sons and daughters are also the inheritors of the deceased's property.

3. But in the absence any of ascendants or descendants the brother and the sister of the deceased will be the inheritors and each of them will get one sixth share of the deceased's property. If they are more than two then they all will be entitled to one-third equally. There is no difference in the share of brother and sister (Begum, 2015, pp. 134-135).

According to Universal declaration of Human Rights adopted by United Nation Organization in 1948, right to marriage is deemed to be one of the fundamental human rights. It maintains that men and women, after they attain maturity, have a right to get married and form family. The marriage can be contracted with the full and free consent of the spouses. Such a right to marriage is in full accord with Islāmic law of marriage. Marriage is contractual as per Islāmic law. Marriage is solemnized after two consenting adults enter into a contract. Both spouses can stipulate their respective conditions. With a view to contracting a marriage both consenting males and females have equal status in the actual execution of a marriage contract. Islām regards a woman to be a free agent with regard to execution of marriage. Her consent is essential to the validation of the marital contract. In fact, Islām does not allow execution of marriage without the consent of an intending female adult. A tradition of the Prophet is reported by Abu Hurairah: The messenger of Allah said,

> A woman without her husband shall not be married till she gives consent nor a virgin be married till her consent is sought. They asked: What shall

count as her permission? He said: If she remains silent (Karim, 2006, p. 611).

It is reported that a girl came to the Prophet of Islām and complained that her father married her to a person without her consent, the Prophet thereupon said to the girl:

> If you do not like this marriage then you are free. She said: I uphold my father's decision but I complained to you to tell other girls and women that their fathers have no right to marry them against their will (Khan,, 2001, p. 15).

Thus, in order to execute a marriage, the consent of a woman is obligatory. In case a minor girl is given in marriage by her guardian, the girl after the attainment of maturity is entitled to retain or reject that marriage at her will. A women's consent is essential to the validation of any marital contract whether that of a widow or virgin or a minor girl. It is true that a woman is given into marriage by her guardian, say, by the grandfather or brother. However, they are obliged to select her partner in accordance with her will. No guardian has authority to impose any person upon the girl. Her consent is intrinsically necessary to validate her marriage.

Islām gives to women right to *Maher* as well. It is a free bridal gift which the husband has to give to the wife while the marriage is to be contracted. A marriage between consenting spouses cannot be solemnised unless the *Maher* is paid or fixed. The Qur'ān does not specify any minimum or maximum limit to *Maher*. Normally, it is to be paid in keeping with the financial status of the consenting spouses. However, the bride-to-be can negotiate the terms and conditions of her *Maher* in the given circumstances. The right to *Maher* is introduced in Islām as future security of the women getting married. The *Maher* has to be substantial enough to act as a check against divorce. Besides, it is a token of man's respect for his wife.

Just as marriage can be solemnised by recourse to mutual consent, so it can be dissolved by recourse to mutual consent as well. If spouses cannot lead a happy life together or develop an irreconcilable differences or it is beyond them to live together amicably, Islām allows the dissolution of marriage. Islām deems marriage to be a civil contract entered into by mutual consent of the bride and bridegroom. Both the husband and the wife have right to go in for divorce by recourse to appropriate mechanisms. The husband can repudiate marriage through *talaq* and wife can repudiate the marriage under a form of divorce known as '*khula*'.

However, Islām only permits dissolution of marriage if in certain extreme conditions it becomes absolutely necessary. The dissolution of marriage should be avoided so for as it is possible. The right to divorce is not to be used in haste as apart from the spouses, the families and larger circle of relatives are also involved in it. The Prophet of Islām is reported to have said: "With Allah the most detestable of all lawful things is divorce" ((Karim, 2006, p. 660).

Furthermore, women also have been given right to maintenance by Islām. While women are married to men and carry out their numerous duties, it is for men to provide them with food, clothing and housing and other facilities. However, in case of divorce the husband has to provide maintenance to his wife under specified conditions. The husband is obliged to treat his wife with kindness. He is obliged to bear the burden of maintenance of his wife. The husband is obliged to provide maintenance to his wife even if she is rich and wealthy enough to carry on her life. The husband is bound to provide maintenance to his wife even after divorce. The divorced woman is entitled to maintenance during the period of *Iddah*. The divorced woman, if pregnant is entitled to maintenance till she lays down her burden.

> Let the women live (in *iddat*) in the same style as ye live, according to your means: Annoy them not, so as to restrict them. And if they carry (life in their wombs), then spend (your substance) on them until they deliver their burden: And if they suckle your (offspring), give them their recompense: And take mutual counsel together, according to what is just and reasonable. And if ye find yourselves in difficulties, let another woman suckle (the child) on the (father's) behalf (*Al-Qur'ān:* 65:6).

She is entitled to maintenance for a period of two years if she agrees to give suck to the child after delivery. There are verses in the Qur'ān which indicate that women are entitled to maintenance even after they have been divorced. The following verse of the Qur'ān as translated by Abdullah Yusuf Ali merits, serious legal consideration: "For divorced women maintenance (should be provided) on a reasonable (scale). This is a duty on the righteous" (Ibid, 2:241).

It seems that the Qur'ān provides maximum possible latitude with regard to maintenance of a divorced woman. The divorced woman is entitled to unqualified maintenance from the husband who has divorced her. Of course, under no category of maintenance, has the Qur'ān anywhere specified the quantum of maintenance. What has been underlined everywhere is the provision of reasonable maintenance. The husband or the ex-husband is obliged to provide maintenance to his wife or ex-wife on a reasonable scale. He has to pay the maintenance to the best of his capability.

A woman in Islām has also been granted the right to employment. Women, like men, can hold any job. They have been granted freedom of economic pursuit. They can serve as teachers, doctors, nurses, writers, lawyers, journalists, etc. They can pursue any trade or commercial activity. They can express their talent and utilize it for the welfare of the society. Like men, women have been allowed to earn their wages. Women, like men, are entitled to the fruits of their labour. The following verse of the Qur'ān is pertinent or apt in this regard: "To men is allotted what they earn, and to women what they earn: But ask Allah of His bounty for Allah hath full knowledge of all things" (Ibid, 4:32). The Qur'ān always lays stress on legitimate earning. What men and women earn by their own labour is legitimate.

It seems to be the case that Islām drastically brings about a revolution in the conditions of women. In almost all previous civilizations, women did not seem to matter much. Their existence was not even acknowledged. In fact, they were hardly treated as human beings. Islām accorded women the right to take their own decisions in every department of their lives. They got the right to education. They got the right to choose their spouses. They got the right to property through inheritance, *mahr* and maintenance. They got the right to utilize their property as and when they deemed it fit. They got the right to get married to a male of their choice. They got the right to give or get divorce in case they find themselves trapped into an unhappy marital relationship. Thus, with the advent of Islām women got the right to education, right to get married to a person of their choice, right to own maintenance and utilize their property and the right to divorce their spouses as and when warranted by unacceptable circumstances. Most importantly, Islām accorded women the right to take their own decisions in various fields of operation. The right to take decisions through mutual consultation as ordained by the Qur'ān was accorded to women as well. In fact, the wives of the Prophet such as Ayesah and Umm Salmah were deemed to be authorities on Islāmic jurisprudence (khan, 1991, p. 53).

Apart from social, political economic and legal status enjoyed by women in Islām, there was need to be cognizant of their moral and the spiritual status as well. The Qur'ān and the *Sunnah* of the Prophet accorded highest moral and spiritual status to women. Take, for example, the status of mother in Islām. The mothers in Islām are placed next to Allah and His Messenger. The Prophet is reported to have said: "Paradise lies under the feet of mother" (Karim, 2006, p. 187). The Qur'ān exhorts to man to accord highest respect to his parents and be fair, kind and obedient to them. The Qur'ān says:

> Thy Lord hath decreed that ye worship none but Him, and that ye be kind to parents. Whether one or both of them attain old age in thy life, say not to them a word of contempt, nor repel them, but address them in terms of honor. And, out of kindness, lower to them the wing of humility, and say: "My Lord! Bestow on them Thy Mercy even as they cherished me in childhood (*Al-Qur'ān:* 17:23-24).

However, the Qur'ān exhorts to respective offsprings to be more kind and obedient toward mothers, for it is mother who bears the brunt of reproduction and bears the offsprings in their wombs in great pain and suffering and also experience highest suffering during the process of delivery. Mothers also experience great pain while bringing up their kids. In view of the same, the Qur'ān says:

> And We have enjoined on man (to be good) to his parents: In travail upon travail did his mother bear him, and in years twain was his weaning: (Hear the command), "Show gratitude to Me and to thy parents: To Me is (thy final) Goal (Ibid, 31:14).

In another verse, the Qur'ān brings out:

> We have enjoined on man kindness to his parents: In pain did his mother bear him, and in pain did she give him birth. The carrying of the (child) to his weaning is (a period of) thirty Months (Ibid, 46:15).

In a reported tradition of the Prophet, mothers are given priority over fathers three times more (Yahya, 1999, p. 294, no.316). In another tradition of the Prophet it is stated that good treatment to the mother is an expiation of a great sin committed by man (Chaudhury, 2006, p. 2). In another tradition, service to mother is deemed to be a higher virtue than participating in a battle or paradise lies in the feet of the mother (Ibid, p. 3). In yet another tradition, believers are asked to accord respect and fair treatment to their mothers even if they are polytheists (Yahya, 1999, p. 301, no.325).

These traditions of the Prophet clearly and categorically establish that women as mothers have been accorded highest status in Islām.

Secondly, women as wives have also been accorded very high status in Islām. The wives are not be subjected to subordination and servitude. They are to be accorded love and affection by their spouses. Women have an independent personality of their own and are not to get dissolved in the personality of their husbands. She can inherit property from her parents, spouses, sons, and also enjoy privileges of maintenance. However, a wife is not merely entitled to legal rights only. Men are asked by the Qur'ān to accord loving and affectionate behaviour to their spouses. They are to be treated on an equal footing. Even if they have some limitations, Allah can compensate for them in other respects as well. The following verse of Qur'ān brings out the same:

> On the contrary live with them on a footing of kindness and equity. If ye take a dislike to them, it may be that ye dislike a thing, and Allah brings about through it a great deal of good (*Al-Qur'ān*: 4:19).

The spousal relationship in Islām is a relationship of love and affection. The loving relationship of husband and wife is recognized in the Qur'ān as one of the signs of Allah. The Qur'ān says:

> And among His Signs is this, that He created for you mates from among yourselves, that ye may dwell in tranquillity with them, and He has put love and mercy between your (hearts): Verily in that are Signs for those who reflect (Ibid, 30:21).

The Qur'ān also brings out the husband-wife relationship in the following words: "they are your garments and you are their garments" (Ibid, 2:187).

With reference to the status of women in Islām, the permission to men to marry upto four wives, is cited by critics as an instance of the degradation of women in Islāmic society or as a violation of their dignity as wives and as human beings. It is true that the Qur'ān permitted Muslim men to marry upto four wives with a view to taking care of the widows and orphans against the backdrop of large-scale killing of warriors during the battle of Ohd. Under the given circumstances, the Muslims were allowed to marry upto four wives with the stipulation that they can do justice to all of them. Polygamy is permitted in Islām with a view to doing justice with widows and orphans. The following verse of the Qur'ān illustrates the issue under consideration:

> If ye fear that ye shall not be able to deal justly with the orphans, marry women of your choice, two, or three, or four; but if ye fear that ye shall not be able to deal justly (with them), then only one, or (a captive) that your right hands possess. That will be more suitable, to prevent you from doing injustice (Ibid, 4:3).

In the light of the above verse of the Qur'ān, it can be said that the permission to practice polygamy in Islām was given to men so as to look after the interests of widows and orphans. The permission was not given to satisfy the personal desires of male believers of the community. The purpose of polygamy was to give shelter to the widows and to take care of the orphans. Thus, polygamy was permitted within a given context. It was not introduced as a general rule. It is the monogamy which is advanced as a general rule and polygamy is allowed to meet out the contingencies under specific conditions. Ghulam ahmad parvez has commented upon polygamy as follows:

> It would be seen that the permission for more than one wife is contingent on two conditions:
>
> (1) If there is an excess of single or husbandless women in society and there is no other reasonable solution possible, then exception could be made to the rule of monogamy and one would marry these (husbandless) women.
>
> (2) This permission is also conditional on justice being done to all individuals in the family. Also, it should be possible for an individual to bear the burden of all the children begotten by the wives. It should not become an unbearable burden on him (Engineer, 2008, p. 122).

However, it should be readily admitted that the provision of polygamy has been grossly misused by countless men across history and globe. What was allowed by the Qur'ān on conditions of equity and justice was misused by Muslims, leading to gross injustice and inequity.

There are critics who bring out that Muslim men keep their women in veil and thus curtail their participation in social, political and economic matters. Such a curtailment is a gross violation of women's social, political and economic rights, which adds upto gross injustice to women. However, such an interpretation of the institution of veil prevalent among Muslim societies is both unnecessary and uncalled for. The veil as it is put on by Muslim women is not necessarily ordained by the Qur'ānic injunctions or traditions of the Prophet. The institution of veil is an outcome of social, political and economic developments across Muslim history. In the prevailing and ongoing historical circumstances, numerous Muslim scholars were convinced of the Islāmic validity and social necessity of putting on veil by Muslim women. However, it is not explicitly recommended by the Qur'ān or by any specific tradition of the Prophet. The Qur'ān has asked Muslim women to put on covering garments on their bodies so that their dignity and modesty is safeguarded. However, Islām has not recommended *Burqua* or *Hijjab* covering feet, hands and faces of women this preventing them from participating in social, political and economic matters. The fundamental value or norm underlined by the Qur'ān is the protection of the dignity and modesty of both Muslim men and women. The following verse of the Qur'ān is specifically addressed to Muslim men:

> Say to the believing men that they should lower their gaze and guard their modesty: That will make for greater purity for them: And Allah is well-acquainted with all that they do (*Al-Qur'ān*: 24:30).

In this verse, Muslim men are obliged to safeguard their modesty. They are asked to cast down their gaze while looking at women. Muslim men are prohibited from looking at women lustfully and are instructed to cast their glances downwards. Similarly, Muslim women are addressed by the Qur'ān in following manner:

> And say to the believing women that they should lower their gaze and guard their modesty; that they should not display their beauty and ornaments except what (must ordinarily) appear thereof; that they should draw their veils over their bosoms and not display their beauty except to their husbands, their fathers, their husbands' fathers, their sons, their husbands' sons, their brothers or their brothers' sons, or their sisters' sons, or their women, or the slaves whom their right hands possess, or male servants free of physical needs, or small children who have no sense of the shame of sex; and that they should not strike their feet in order to draw attention to their hidden ornaments. And O ye Believers! Turn ye all together towards Allah, that ye may attain Bliss (Ibid, 24:31).

Thus, both men and women are asked by the Qur'ān to safeguard their modesty and not indulge in immoral activities.

Muslim scholars have always differed on the exact meaning of what constitutes the veil. For example, according to Ibn Abbas, hands and the faces of women need not be covered by the veil. Abdullah-bin- Masud, on the other hand, held that hands and faces of women can also not be exposed. The Prophet of Islām is reported to have instructed Asma bint Abu Bakr that except their faces and hands all the other body parts of ladies should be covered by an outer garment. There is another verse in the Qur'ān which reads as follows:

> O Prophet! Tell thy wives and daughters, and the believing women, that they should cast their outer garments over their persons (when abroad): That is most convenient, that they should be known (as such) and not molested. And Allah is Oft-Forgiving, Most Merciful (Ibid, 33:59).

No verse of the Qur'ān prescribes believing women to cover their faces and hands as such. What's underlined by the Qur'ānic verses is that women should dress in a dignified manner. The women are advised to dress in a dignified manner. Their dresses should be in white or inspire ill-conduct or lead to corruption of the society. The women are advised to dress in a dignified manner while they are outside of their houses especially at market places. The Qur'ān also asks believing women not to display their beauty before strangers. So they are advised to cover their bodies properly and especially draw veils on their bosoms once they step outside their homes. The purpose of such an instruction given by the Qur'ān to women is to protect their chastity. It is not meant to confine women to four walls of their homes. Nor it is the purpose of the Qur'ān to impose a uniform dress code on women as is insisted by the traditional theologians. No dress code should be imposed on Muslim women which operates as a roadblock in their educational, cultural, intellectual, social, political and economic progress.

The above discussion with regard to women's status in Islām should illustrate the fact that the rights accorded to women by the Qur'ān and the *Sunnah* constitute an exceptional breakthrough in the historical struggle of women for equality, dignity and justice. The Qur'ān is in accord with contemporary feminist quest for equality and gender justice. It is the historical circumstances emerging after the advent of Islām which have led to patriarchy and degradation of women. It is the feudal history of Muslims that led to rigid veil system and wide-spread practice of polygamy among Muslims. It is the feudal system which led to the subordination of women by men. It is the feudal system which promoted patriarchal norms and established male chauvinism. Patriarchal and male chauvinistic values distorted the truth of Islām. Consequently, Islām came to be recognized as leading to bondage of women. The Qur'ān as such underlines gender equality and gender justice. The following verse of the Qur'ān testifies to the same:

> For Muslim men and women, --for believing men and women, for devout men and women, for true men and women, for men and women who are patient and constant, for men and women who humble themselves, for men and women who give in charity, for men and women who fast (and deny themselves), for men and women who guard their chastity, and for men and women who engage much in Allah's praise, --for them has Allah prepared forgiveness and great reward (Ibid, 33:35).

The Qur'ān and the *Sunnah* have advocated women's emancipation and empowerment. However, as Muslims have been largely ignorant of the basic sources of Islām and as women have been denied education and awareness by Muslim society, it is in consequence of these factors that Muslim women find themselves in deplorable conditions. It is Muslims who owing to various social, political and economic factors could not execute the Islāmic revolution in its proper spirit and perspective. The historical factors of Muslims should not be ascribed to Islāmic worldview and value system. What's needed is proper education and enlightenment of both Muslim men and women so that Islāmic values and norms can become instrumental in the onward march of Muslim emancipation and transformation.

2.7 SLAVERY IN ISLĀM

The institution of slavery is as old as human history itself. Slavery has been practiced across history and throughout the globe. Ancient Babylonians, Egyptians, Romans, Greeks, Turks, Persians, Indians, Chinese, etc had large populations as slaves. In recent history black Africans were purchased as slaves by Euro-Americans on a very large scale. For various social, political, economic and ideological reasons, slavery has existed in some form or the other throughout human history.

Islām emerged in early seventh century and established itself across North Africa, West Asia, Central Asia and parts of Eastern and Southern Europe within the first half of seventh century. It confirmed almost all the previous religions and yet in many respects it can be seen as revolutionary breakthrough. Islām emerged in the Arab society comprised of masters and slaves. The institution of slavery was widespread, almost all-pervasive across Northern Africa, West Asia, Central Asia, European continent and large parts of Southern and Eastern Asia. Islām did not establish or connive at the institution of slavery. Islām confronted the problem of slavery. It is true that in the thousands of verses of the Qur'ān the practice of the slavery is nowhere proscribed. But neither is it prescribed. The Qur'ān could have legally banned the practice of slavery. However, in His unqualified Wisdom, Allah chooses exhortative rather than a legislative approach. One possible explanation of this approach is that thousands of slaves had no wherewithal to lead independent lives. They had no material or economic resources to fend for themselves. They were on the mercy of their masters. With a view to liberating the slaves and establishing them on their own, a conciliatory rather than a confrontationist approach was indispensable. Allah persuaded the believers to set the slaves free. It is reported that the Prophet of Islām himself set free as many as sixty three slaves. His wife Ayesha liberated sixty seven slaves, his uncle Abbas liberated seventy slaves, Abd Allah Ibn Umar liberated one thousand slaves etc. Other companions of the Prophet purchased thousands and thousands of slaves and set them free (Slavery in Islām, 2013, p. 11, www. Islāmreligion.com website). It is reported that within less than half a century the institution of slavery fizzled out in Arabia for all practical purposes.

However, what's more important is that Islām accorded the best possible treatment to slaves. The foremost antidote against slavery was the categorical proclamation by the Qur'ān and by the Prophet of Islām that all human beings are equal in origin and destiny. The Qur'ān declares:

> O mankind! We created you from a single (pair) of a male and a female, and made you into nations and tribes, that ye may know each other (not that ye may despise each other). Verily the most honored of you in the sight of Allah is (he who is) the most righteous of you. And Allah has full knowledge and is well acquainted (with all things) (*Al-Qur'ān:* 49:13).

The Prophet of Islām said: "All of you are from Adam and Adam was created from dust" (Slavery in Islām, 2013, p. 8).The Prophet of Islām also educated the believers with regard to slaves in the following words:

> Your slaves are your brothers! God has placed them in your care. So, whose brother is under his care, he should feed him what he eats and dress him how he dresses. And do not burden them beyond their capacities; but if you burden them (with an unbearable burden), then help them (by sharing their extra burden) (*Saheeh Al-Bukhari*). See also (Slavery in Islām, 2013, p. 9).

Islām granted equal religious and civil rights to slaves and accepted their rights to personal belonging and property. It asked believers to set slaves free with a view to atoning for their sins and acts of transgression. Muslims were assured that setting slaves free can save them from the torment of hellfire. The Qur'ān stipulated that

Zakat or obligatory charity given by wealthy Muslims can be spent on setting slaves free as well.

2.8 CONCEPT OF LABOUR IN ISLĀM

Islām does not question the traditional ownership rights of lands and properties. Like socialists, it does not promise a classless society and dictatorship of the proletariat. The basic social, political and economic ethos of Islām is premised on equity rather than equality. In fact, it is not proper to exclusively understand Islāmic social, political and economic principles in the light of post-Enlightenment European history in which anti-monarchical struggles led to emergence of liberal values and assumptions, which values and assumptions led to the emergence of capitalist system and a reaction against capitalist system culminated into socialist alternative as primarily pioneered by Karl Marx in nineteenth century Europe. Rather, Islām was revealed in early seventh century in Arab society, where instead of capitalist modes of production and socialist struggles thereof, we find liberal values and modes determining the behavior of Arab society. Islām emerged as a Reform Movement in Arabia. It did not question the then prevailing assumptions of Arab economy. It accepted the prevailing ownership rights. However, it introduced certain policy measures which could, in course of time transform the economic conditions of down-trodden sections of the society, especially slaves and labourers. Besides, and more importantly, Islām tried to change the basic ethos of believers by injecting in them a world-view and a value-system which could iron out the imbalances and injustices prevalent at that point of human history. The Qur'ānic verses and the traditions of the Prophet, besides offering legal provisions, also offered exhortative considerations with a view to ameliorating the conditions of the working class. Take, for example, the following:

With regard to labours, the fundamental teaching of Islām is not to impose on them any work-load that is beyond their capacity. They should be provided with a humane working system. The workers should not be overtaxed by undue work-load. According to Ibn Hazam, "It is proper for the owner to extract as much work from the worker as he can do and which lies within the ambit of his capacity. No one be forced to do what the latter cannot withstand". There is reported tradition of the Prophet who said: "Do not tax the labour with work that is beyond his power" (Toseef, 2005, p. 100).

The following *Hadīth Qudsi* brings out the relationship between the employer and employees:

> Your brethren are your servants whom Allah has made your subordinate. So, then a man who has his brother as his subordinate should give him to eat what he himself eats, and to wear what he himself wears. And do not put on them the burden of any labour that may exhaust them. And if you have to put any such burden on them, then help them yourselves (in his work) (Ibid, 2005, p. 101).

The Qur'ān says:

> Is it they who would portion out the Mercy of thy Lord? It is We Who portion out between them their livelihood in the life of this world: And We raise some of them above others in ranks, so that some may command work from others. But the Mercy of thy Lord is better than the (wealth) which they amass (*Al-Qur'ān*: 43:32).

In another *Hadith Qudsi* it is said:

> The person who has been assigned some work by us, must get a house if he does not have one, he must get married if he has no wife, he must get a conveyance if he has none (Toseef, 2005, p. 108).

The Prophet said: "The prophet commanded that quick payment should be made before worker's sweat has become dry" (Ibid, p. 116).

Islām is fundamentally against any economic system in which employers can exploit their employees. It exhorts employers to create an environment of justice, equity and harmony while undertaking any productive activity. The wages of labourers should be fixed fairly and justly i.e. equivalent to the job done. Most importantly, the employees and employers should cooperate with one another in keeping with the theological directives and eschatological imperatives of Islām.

REFERENCES

1. Numani, A. R. (1986). *Lughat-ul-Qur'ān.* Vol. IV, Karachi: Darul Ishat Publisher.

2. Gibb, H. A. R. (1979). (Ed.). *Encyclopedia of Islām.* Vol. I, London: New York.

3. Maūdudī, A. A. (2014). *Takhees Tafheem-ul-Qur'ān.* New Delhi: Markazi Maktaba Islāmi Publisher.

4. Khadduri, M. (1984). *The Islāmic Conception of Justice.* Baltimore and London: The Johns Hopkins University Press.

5. Bernstein, S. B. (2009). *Reading the Qur'ānic Conception (s) of Justice.* (Un-Published thesis of Bachelor of Arts). Wesleyan University.

6. Qureshi, T. A. (1982). *Justice in Islām.* Islāmic Studies, 21 (2).

7. Malik, I. (1951). *Muwatta 2:720 (Kitab Al-Aqdiyah).*

8. Ali, A. Y. (2007). *The Holy Qur'ān.* New Delhi: Islāmic Book Service.

9. Sharif, M. M. (2001). *A History of Muslim Philosophy.* Vol. I, Delhi: Adam Publishers and Distributors.

10. *Prophet Muhammad's Last Sermon* (2013). (www.Islāmreligion. Com website.

11. Ahmad, K. & Hassan, A. (2003). *Distributive Justice: the Islāmic Perspective.* Intellectual Discourse, 8 (2).

12. Imām, K. *Zakat in Islām: Conceptualization, Categorization & Ruling.* (http://docplayer.net/35900031-Zakat-in-Islām-conceptualization categorization-ruling.html).

13. Karim, M. F. (2006). *Al-Hadith, Mishkat-ul-Masabih.* Vol. I, New Delhi: Islāmic book service.

14. Maūdudī, A. A. (1982). *Human Rights in Islām.* Delhi: Markazi Maktaba Islāmic.

15. *Al-Hadith, Muslim Sharif, Kitabul-Hajj,*

16. Ali, P. S. (1995). *Human Rights in Islām*. New Delhi: Adam Publishers and Distributors.

17. Hussain, S. S. (1991). *Human Rights in Islām*. Malaysia: Darual Ehsaan.

18. Mahmood, T. (1993). (Ed.). *Human Rights in Islām*. New Delhi: Genuine Publications Private Ltd.

19. Mawdudi, A. A. (1969). *The Islāmic Law and Constitution*. Lahore: Islāmic Publication Ltd.

20. *Al-Hadith, Miskhat, KitabulIlm*.

21. Al-Minwai, K. M. (1993). *Human Rights in Islām*. Al-Madina_al-Munawarah: King Fahd Holy Qur'ān Printing Complex.

22. *Al-Hadith, Nisaai*. Vol. VII, darul-Kitab, Beirut,

23. Shamsi, N. (2003). *Human Rights in Islām*. New Delhi: EssEss Publication.

24. Hussain, S. S. (1991). *Islām and Human Rights*. Malaysia: Budaya Ilmu Sdn. Bhd.

25. *Universal Islāmic Declaration of Human Rights,* From Article 1st to 20th. Dhul Qaidah 1401, 1981).

26. *Cairo Declaration on Human Rights in Islām,* Aug. 5, 1990, U.N. GAOR.

27. De Preux, J. (1994). *Geneva Convention III: relative to the treatment of prisoners of war: Commentary*. International committee of Red Cross.

28. Lawson, E. (1995). *Encyclopedia of Human Rights*. Washington, DC.

29. Patwari, M. I. *Human Rights in international Law and Islāmic Law, A Comparison.*

30. Khan, M. H. (1991). *The Schools of Islāmic Jurisprudence*. New Delhi: Kitab Bhavan.

31. Begum, S. S. (2015). *The Status of Women and the Concept of Justice in Islām*. (Un-Published Ph. D Thesis). Gauhati University.

32. Khan, M. S. (2001). *Status of women in Islām*. New Delhi: A. P. H. Publishing Corporation.

33. Yahya, Al-Imām A. Z. (1999). *Riyad-us-Saliheen*. Vol. I, Riyadh: Daussalam Publisher & Distributors.

34. Chaudhury, M. S. (2006). *Women's Right in Islām*. New Delhi: Adam Publishers and Distributors.

35. Engineer, A. A. (2008). *The Rights of Women in Islām*. New Delhi: Sterling Publishers Limited.

36. *Slavery in slam,* (2013). See also
https://d1.Islāmhouse.com/data/en/ih_articles/single2/en_Slavery_in_Islām.pdf

37. Azid, T. (2005). *The Concept and Nature of Labour in Islām: A Survey*. Review of Islāmic Economics, 9 (2).

CHAPTER-III

REVIEW OF THE CONCEPT OF JUSTICE IN CLASSICAL MUSLIM PHILOSOPHY

3.1 THE KHAWARIJ

Sunnīs and Shī'ahs are two principal parties who emerged, of course, in post Muhammadan era i.e. after 632 A.D. While seeds of Shī'ah-Sunnī sectarianism were sown just after the Prophet's demise, it was only after the tragedy at Karbala that Shī'ahs and Sunnī were polarized into doctrinally and theologically opposed camps. Although both these sects believed in One Supreme God, His Angels, His Books, His Prophets, Day of Judgment, Resurrection, Determination of good and evil by God etc, they mainly differed as to the locus of successorship.

Apart from Sunnīs and Shī'ahs there arose a politically significant group of Muslims who were equally opposed to Sunnīs and Shī'ahs. In fact they cursed both the majority Sunnīs and Shī'ahs or partisans of Ali. There were doctrinal and political rebels. The Khawarijites originated from their opposition to agreement between Hazrat Ali and his challenger Muawiyah who was a kinsman of the third Caliph Uthman, Who was martyred by the rebels. Some of the Ali's followers, mostly from the Arab tribe Tamim, advanced the view that any arbitration between the camps of Muawiyah and Ali amounted to commission of a great sin and accordingly, Ali cannot be considered to be a Muslim, Consequently, they made an exodus *(Khuruj)* from the camp of Ali and were designated as Kharijis (those who made exodus). The Khawarijis were deeply committed to one of the fundamental values enshrined into the Qur'ān and *Sunnah:* equality of all Muslims without a regard to race, tribe, color etc. In view of the same, non-Arabs were greatly attracted to the camps of khawarijis (Eliade, 1987, p. 288). According to Shahrastani:

> Whoever rebelled against the legitimate *Imām* accepted by the people is called a Kharijite, whether this rebellion took place at the time of the companions against the rightfully guided *Imām*, or against their worthy successors, or against the *Imāms* of anytime (Shahrastani, 1984, P. 98).

The emergence of the Khawarij gave rise to an early major issue of *Kalām*, namely the status and fate of *murtakib al-kabirah:* whether committing a grave sin makes a person a *kafir* (infidel, to be condemned to Hell fire for ever) or not. Here we find that the Kharijites take the extreme view of considering such a person as an infidel, interpreting in their own way Qur'ānic verses that do not agree with this stand (Hossein & Oliver, 1996, p. 79).

According to Shahratani, the most important groups within Khawarijis were known as the Muhakkimah, the Azariqah, the Baihasiyah, the Ajarida, the Ibadiyya, and the Sufariya (Shahrastani, 1984, p. 99).

In the light of their own political and religious orientation, the khawarijis put up a great struggle against Umayyad Caliphs. However, they could not succeed in dislodging them, for the majority of Muslims were not prepared to support their views. The khawarijis to begin with, emerged as a political force, and in course of time, they also developed into a religious group. The following are the guiding principles of Khawarijis:

1. The Caliph must be elected and be responsible to Muslims. He needs not to be of the Quraish descent. Any Muslim even a slave, can be elected and remain *Khalifa*, so long as the people were satisfied with his rule; if not, he might be deposed or even killed. Some extremists among them did not like to have any common head and were content with a dictator whenever they needed.

2. A Muslim who does not perform regularly his prayers and observe the fasts and other rituals is no better than a *Kafir* (infidel).

3. A Muslim, if he has committed a sin and dies without repentance, deserves eternal punishment in Hell.

4. All those Muslims who do not agree with Kharijites ought to be considered as infidels, whom the Kharijites must fight and destroy (Shushtery, 1938, p. 551).

5. They acknowledged Abu Bakr and Umar as Rightful Caliphs but Uthman, in their opinion, had, towards the end of his reign, erred from the Path of justice and right conduct and hence deserved to be deposed or killed. Ali also committed, according to them, a major sin when he accepted the arbitration of "one besides God". The two arbiters (Amr ibn As and abu Musa al-Ash'arī), their choosers (Ali and Muawiyah), and all those who agreed to arbitration were sinners. All those who participated in the battle of the Camel including Talhah, Zubair, and Aishah, the Prophet's wife, had been guilty of grievous sin.

6. The Qur'ān was recognized as the authoritative source of Law but their views on *Hadith* (the Prophet's Tradition) and *ijma* (the agreement of Muslims in respect of a rule of law) were different from those of the majority.

7. Sin, with the Khawarij, was synonymous with infidelity. Anyone who committed a major sin (and did not repent and revert) was placed outside the pale of Islām. All the personages mentioned above were declared infidels Anathema was pronounced against them, and they were considered fit to be censured. The Muslims in general were pronounced infidels, first, because they were not free from sins, and, secondly, because they not only regarded these persons as Muslims but also acknowledged them as reliable guides, and deduced and verified the law from traditions reported by them.

8. The Caliph, according to them, should be elected by the free vote of the Muslims.

9. The Caliph need not be a member of the tribe of Quraish. Whomsoever they elected from amongst the honest Muslims would be a rightful Caliph.

10. A Caliph was to be obeyed faithfully as long as he acted rightly and justly; but if he forsook the path of righteousness and justice, he was to be fought against and deposed or assassinated (Sharif, 2001, p. 668).

A group of Khawarijis known as Al-Najdiyyah questioned the very need of a State. They underlined that Muslims should conduct themselves righteously without establishing a State. In case, they need Caliph to guide them; they can choose one through an appropriate and consensual arrived method. The Azariqah sect of Khawarijites was the most hard core group among the Khawarijites. They believed that only they were authentic Muslims and all other sects across the board were polytheists. All other Muslim Religious groups were to be fought against till they accepted the Khawarijite doctrines. Unless they concurred with Khawarijis interpretation of Divine Justice, it was obligatory on Muslims to fight against them, till their women and children and loot their property. Even these Khawarijis were also infidels who did not put up an unrelenting war against non- Khawarij Muslims.

However there were some tolerant people among them as well. They were Ibadiyyah. They did not deem other Muslims to be as polytheists. However they declared them to be outside the pale of Islam and designated them as unbelievers. They did approve of secret assaults on other Muslims although they considered open warfare with other Muslims to be a legitimate duty.

In the light of approach appropriated by Khawarijis, it can be concluded that they advanced what may be called Retributive theory of justice.

3.2 THE MURJIA

The Murjia as a political and religious movement in early Islām can be contrasted with the Khawarijis. As against Khawarijis, the Murjis identified faith with belief or confession of belief. A person was Muslim if he or she authentically believed in God, institution of the Prophethood and such eschatological events as resurrection and the Day of Judgment. The implication is that confession of faith is necessary and sufficient condition for being a Muslim. Of course, right conduct was central to Islamic teachings. Man is asked to refrain from both *Kabirah* (great sin) and *Saghirah* (small sin). However, no human being or any group of human beings has the right to declare any one to be infidel. Such words as Murjia and *Irja* having derived from Qur'ānic word *'Arja'* mean the deferment of judgment. Another related meaning of the word *'Arja'* is 'to give hope' (Bosworth, 1993, p. 605). Shahrastani writes,

> One of the meanings of al-*irja* is deferring the case of one who commits a grave sin to the Day of Judgement; in this world, therefore, no judgement is made as to whether he belongs to the people of Paradise or the people of Hell (Shahrastani, 1984, p.119).

The Murjis are comprised of four groups: the Khawarijite Murjia, the Qadarite Murjia, the Jabarite Murjia and pure Murjia (Ibid). According to Abdul Qahir of Baghdad, the Murjis can be classified in three ways:

1. A group of Murjis believed in Islām and were free williest such as Ghailan of Damascus, Abu-Shamvi, and Muhammad, son of Abu Shabib of Basra.
2. There were other Murjis who were faithful believers but were Jabarites, for they held that man is not bestowed with freedom of will.
3. Another group of Murjis held faith as most essential and above actions. They believed faith to be pre-eminent to actions. Imām Abu Hanifa may be cited as a prominent Murji following this sect. According to Imām Abu Hanifa no Muslim will be consigned to eternal hellfire. A person is a Muslim if he expresses the articles of faith through his tongue and believes then in his heart (Sushtery, 1938, p. 552). According to Sharistani, every sin will be surely forgiven except polytheism (Shahrastani, 1984, p.120). There were others who held that a Muslim cherishing faith in his heart remains a Muslim and entitled to paradisal bliss even if he worships Idols or adopts Jews and Christian doctrines (Ibid pp. 122-123). However, there were disagreements amongst Murjis themselves.

There were some Murjis who accepted that Muslims were duty-bound, according to the Qur'ān to fight for what is righteous *(Ma'ruf)* and fight against what is vicious *(Munkar)*. However in the given contexts we need to avoid such a trial. It was obligatory on Muslims to check others on wrong conduct. However, Muslims should not put up any fight against tyranny of government. A prominent Murji al-Jassas was highly embittered with regard to such an ethical and political stand taken by Murjis. He thought that such a stand is deeply demoralizing to such Muslims who want to put up resistance against the forces of evil and wickedness (Sharif, 2001, p. 670).

The fundamental principles of Murjis may be tabled as hereunder:

1. Muslims must worship and serve God alone and must not associate any being with him.

2. All Muslims are members of Islam.

3. All non-Muslims are equal in their wrong beliefs.

4. Doubtful questions such as disagreement between the early companions, and the claims of several men for the office of *Khilafat*, etc, must be left to Divine judgement. Those companions, whom the Muslim public consider sinners, may be forgiven by God or in truth may not be guilty, though misunderstood by others.

5. A Muslim must not fight against a Muslim, except in self-defence.

6. Good intention, though followed by wrong action, will have its own reward.

7. God's will is above human will.

8. The first four Caliphs were all-good. (This statement is against the Kharijite idea, who denied the third and the fourth Caliphs).

9. Man must be judged by God alone for punishment or reward.

10. The apparent submission to the laws of Islam with no faith in Islām is of no use.

11. If there is faith, sins may be forgiven, except *shirk* (infidelity) (Sushtery,1938, p. 552).

The Murjis stand on justice is diametrically opposed to Khawarij stand. The Murjis hold that 'great sinner' *(Murtakibul Kabirah)* too are Muslims and not outside the pale of Islam, for our actions are not integral to faith. Sins do not disqualify a believer from being a Muslim. Just as good deeds cannot qualify an infidel to be a Muslim. They advanced such as view in light of Qur'ānic verses promising good future for the believers. However, they interpreted those verses of the Qur'ān that threaten punishment to wrong-doers to suit their own position. Many leading scholars among the companions of the Prophet (*Suhabah*) and the companions of companions (*Tabiun*) were largely attracted to Murjites interpretation of the Qur'ānic verses. They underlined that a sinning believer remains a Muslim. The destiny of the sinner is best left to God who may pardon him or her or accord the proper punishment He deems (Nasr & Oliver, 1996, p.79). There is a feel of eschatological optimism in stand taken by Murjis. The sinner nurses an existential hope for forgiveness. So, they may be said to be advancing an optimistic or existential theory of justice.

3.3 THE JABRIYAH

Philosophers of religion or philosophical theologians have always been discussing or debating the question of free will and determinism. This problem is more pronounced in Semitic religions such as Judaism, Christianity and Islām. These religions rest on the horns of dilemma. They assign Absolute Sovereignty to God and yet insist on unqualified responsibility of man. The Qur'ān features verses on both Absolute Sovereignty of God and complete responsibility of man for his actions. In view of the same, various philosophical and theological groups at the very outset espoused either complete determinism or complete libertarianism. Some of these groups try to appropriate the middle path, leading to various reconciliatory or qualificatory statements with regard to both unqualified Divine Sovereignty and fully-fledged human pre-destination. The earliest philosophical and theological groups who espoused unqualified predestinarianism were known as Murjites and Jabarites. Those who advocated complete human freedom were known as Qadarites and subsequently designated as Mu'tazilites. Both these groups cited extensively from the Qur'ān in support of their respective standpoints. The Qadarites underlined that human will is completely free and Jabarites advanced the view that human will is absolutely determined. The Qadarite stand indicates that God has no control over our actions and the Jabarite stand amounts to saying that we have no control over our actions (Parrott, 2017, p. 3).

The debate between Jabarites and Qadarites emerged during the very lifetime of the Prophet. The companions of the Prophet would ask him as to whether man has free will or is under complete compulsion (Nasr, & Leaman, 1996, pp. 78-79). In course of time, Predestinarians and Free williests continued to discuss the problem with reference to Qur'ān and the *Sunnah*. The Jabarites as already submitted, were the votaries of unqualified predestinarianism. Sharistani classifies Jabarites into two groups; (1) Pure Jabarites holding man to be incapable of doing any action or partially contributing to any operation undertaken in numerous spheres of the world and (2) Moderate Jabarites who admit that man has some power although it does not culminate into any effective action (Sharistani, 1984, p. 72). Of course, there were others who maintain that human power does have some impact on human action and called it acquisition (*Qasb*) they were called Ash'arites (Ibid).

The Jabarites advanced powerful arguments in support of Absolute Divine Sovereignty and complete predestination. It was relatively easier for them to do so as the Qur'ān features extraordinarily powerful verses upholding Divine Sovereignty and predestinarianism. They cited the following verses of the Qur'ān in support of their contention:

1. He hath power over all things (*Al-Qur'ān*: 11:4).
2. For Allah carries out all that He plans (Ibid, 22:14).
3. For Allah hath power over all things (Ibid, 16:77).
4. Allah creates what He wills (Ibid, 24:45).
5. He forgiveth whom He pleaseth, and punisheth whom He pleaseth. For Allah hath power over all things (Ibid, 2:84).
6. Verily, all things have we created in proportion and measure (Ibid, 54:49).

The Jabarites were subdivided into numerous sects. The prominent among them were (1) The Jahmiya, (2) The Najjariya and (3) The Dirariya.

The Jabarites who followed Jahm b. Safwan are known as Jahmiya. They were pure determinists. According to them, man as he is, is completely shorn or divested of any power. He cannot initiate any action. He has no power, no will and no choice.

God creates actions in man as He creates actions in inanimate objects. We can only metaphorically assign actions to human beings. In reality, whatever is done is done by God (Sharastani, 1984 p. 17).

According to Jahmiya, man is under compulsion and it is God who creates good or bad actions. Man is helplessly working as a machine and in no way responsible for his actions. Some historians have alleged that Jahamiya or other Jabarites were encouraged by Umayyad with a view to justifying their misdeeds. However, such a contention is not authenticated by any neutral or independent account (Nasr & Leaman, 1996, p. 80).

The Najjariya sect was led by Husain b. Muhammad al-Najjar. According to Najjariya all actions whether good or bad, right or wrong etc. have been created by God and man only acquires these actions. Such an acquirement has some impact on human actions. In this regard, they were akin to the stand taken up by Ash'arites (Sharastani, 1984, p. 75).

Another sect known as Darariya were the followers of Dirar b. amr. They also held that human actions are really created by Allah and human beings only acquire these actions. Thus, what we call human actions actually originated from Allah and their acquirement by man imparts some agency to human beings as well. Human actions may be said to be co-produced by God and man (Ibid, p. 76).

The above account with regard to Jabarites shifts the locus of justice to God. If human beings are under compulsion to carry out good or bad actions, according to Divinely designated programme, the question of human freedom of will does arise at all. If human beings are not free to carry out their actions, then they do not deserve either reward or punishment. In view of the same, the question of justice or injustice pales into insignificance. It seems that the creation of the universe including man is worked out in the light of some inscrutable Divine plan. Man cannot fathom such a mystery. He has to accept his destiny as and when it is revealed in afterlife.

3.4 THE QADARIYAH

In contrast to Jabarites, another group named as Qadariya espoused that human beings are fully powerful and capable of carrying out free actions. There were some radical Qadarites who advocated that human beings carry out their actions without any assistance from Allah (Nasr & Leaman. 1996, p. 79). The Qadariya School is reported to have been started by Mabad al-Juhaini (d. 80/699). He was an advocate of *Tafwid,* signifying of action and responsibility to man. The Qadarites underlined that human beings have complete control over their actions.

The Qadarites were exponents of the liberty of human will and action. The radicals among the Qadarites believed man to be invested with Divine powers. He has unqualified control over his actions and was fully free to go in for right and wrong actions. Mabad al-Juhani was deadly opposed to the predestarianism allegedly patronized by Umayyad rulers. Al-Juhaini accused Umayyad of misgovernment and vicious deeds. He also held them responsible for disrupting or dividing the Muslims Commonwealth. In view of these radical views al Juhaini was put death in 80 A.H. by Hajjaj under the instigation of Caliph 'Abdul Malik' son of Marwan. After al-Juhaini's death, Ghilan of Damascus highlighted the standpoint of Qadarites by underling that it was incumbent for believers to enforce what's righteous and to eradicate what's vicious (Nadvi, 2009, pp. 20-21). The Qadarite standpoint was further underlined and galvanized by Hassan al-Basri (d. A.D. 728), who made a significant contribution to the Muslim ethical consciousness. Hassan was convinced that man needs to be having a measure of free will in order to be counted as morally responsible for actions (Donaldson, 1953, p. 98).

Ummayyads, it seems, were appreciative of the doctrine of fatalism for political reasons. After 656 A.D. they were the first dynasty rulers and enjoyed all the pomp and show as a political power. Caliph Abdul Malik and governor Hajjaj asked Hasan al-Basri to explain his views with regard to determinism. Hasan submitted that:

> In the Qur'ān qadar is postulated as complete and absolute determinism, not only physical but ethical and spiritual as well. It deprives man of any initiative, any choice, and any voluntary share in his conduct. Man's destiny can only be what God knew that, by His all embracing Qadar, it would be. Any endeavour on man's own behalf is doomed to fail, his fate having been determined beforehand by God's knowledge and volition. From the very womb of his mother man has been decreed to be blessed or affected without any merit acquired, or any iniquity committed, his breast is made wide and easy or straight and narrow. He is created for hell-fire or paradise, just as he is formed tall or short, black or white. Accordingly he is rewarded for deeds he could not help performing and made to answer for others he had no way of preventing; as when the adulterer is punished for having begotten a child whose birth was, in truth, decreed by

the will of God. Man triumphs or suffers for works done, not by him, but in him, though despite of him (Donaldson, 1953, p. 99).

However Hasan Insisted that man, according to the Qur'ān, is capable of doing in the eyes of Allah. It indicates while God controls all the ontological and existential operations of the cosmos, he does not do so in the sphere of moral conduct. In sphere of human moral struggle God's Decree, His will, His knowledge etc do not do the same as in the sphere of man's physical existence. God explicitly commands in the Qur'ān to do what's good and refrain from what's evil. It indicates that man is blessed with a measure of free will (Donaldson, 1953, pp. 99-100). Hasan al-Basri also argued that what Allah forbids is not from Him. He underlined that Umayyad governors and officials cannot justify their wrong and tyrannical deeds under the pretext of the doctrine of absolute determinism. Allah does not command us to be violent or tyrannical. He does not command abominations. While guidance is from Allah, the abomination is human being who indulged in abomination (Ibid, p. 100).

The Qadarites were suppressed by Umayyad rulers in all possible ways. However they held their own for considerable period of time. Later on, they flourished under the title of Mu'tazilah for several centuries.

The Qadarites advanced their theory of free will on the basis of following verses of Qur'ān which affirm human freedom and responsibility:

1. Whoever works righteousness benefits his own soul; whoever works evil, it is against his own soul: Nor is thy Lord ever unjust (in the least) to His servants (*Al-Qur'ān*: 41:46)

2. Allah is never unjust in the least degree: If there is any good (done), He doubleth it and giveth from His own presence a great reward (Ibid, 4:40).

3. When they do aught that is shameful, they say: "We found our fathers doing so"; and "Allah commanded us thus": Say: "Nay, Allah never commands what is shameful: Do ye say of Allah what ye know not?" (Ibid, 7:28).

4. For each (such person) there are (angels) in succession, before and behind him; they guard him by command of Allah. Verily never will Allah change the condition of a people until they change it themselves (with their own souls). But when (once) Allah willeth a people's punishment, there can be no turning it back, nor will they find, beside Him, any to protect (Ibid, 13:11).

> 5. O ye men! Now Truth hath reached you from your Lord! Those who receive guidance, do so for the good of their own souls; those who stray, do so to their own loss: And I am not (set) over you to arrange your affairs (Ibid, 10:108).

The Qadarites were the first philosophical or theological group who underlined human free will and human responsibility. It is in view of their espousal of freedom and responsibility that they are entitled to, at least, eschatological justice. If they committed vicious deeds they will go to hellfire. And if they performed righteous deeds they will be blessed with paradisal bounty and happiness.

3.5 THE MUTAZILAH

Mu'tazilism is one of the most important philosophical theological schools of early Islām. The emergence of Mu'tazilism can be traced to the debate already carried out by Jabarites and Qadarites on such issues as free will and determinism, role of Reason and Revelation and Divine justice etc. The Mu'tazilites were rationalists and accepted the overriding role of Reason in the understanding and application of revelatory propositions and commandments embodied as in the Qur'ān. Literally speaking, the word 'Mu'tazilite' signifies one who has separated from any group or person. It is reported that while Hasan-al-Basri was delivering his lecture on the status of a great sinner, Wasil ibn Ata stood up and opined that the status of a great sinner can be said to be in between believer and an infidel. Thereafter, he tried illustrate his point to some fellow students in another corner of mask. At this point Hasan al-Basri exclaimed *'Itazalanna,* (he seceded from us). Subsequently, Wasil and his followers were designated as seceders or Mu'tazilites. In course of time Mu'tazilah emerged as one of the most powerful schools of philosophical theology (Sharif, 2001, pp. 199-200). Mu'tazilites were, broadly speaking a group of philosophical theologians who separated from other Muslims on the question of the status of a great sinner in Islām. They advanced the view that a great sinner can be said to be in between faith and unbelief, and intermediate rank *(manzilahbain al-manzilatain).*

Mu'tazilism as a school of philosophical theology posits five basic principles:

1. Unity of God.
2. Justice of God.
3. Predestination and Freewill.

4. The essentiality of Good and Evil Actions.
5. Promise of Reward and Threat of Punishment.

UNITY OF GOD

The Mu'tazilites underlined the unity of God so much so that they denied the separate existence of Divine attributes. Their fundamental contention was that God is One and He has no attributes apart from His Essence. For example, God's Knowledge, Power, Mercy, Love etc. are His attributes, not separate from but integral to His Essence. Mu'tazilites did not completely deny the attributes of God; they only affirmed that all Divine attributes are identical with God's Essence.

THE JUSTICE OF GOD

Another fundamental dogma of Mu'tazilism is the principle of necessary justice. The principle of necessary justice of God is at the heart of Mu'tazilah philosophical theology. More than their commitment to the principle of *Ah-al-Tawhid*, they underscore their identity as *Ahl-ul-adl* (Bosworth, 1993, p. 789). The issue of Divine justice is debated in the context of free will, good and evil, and reward and punishment. Mu'tazilah underlined that God is ever just and can never be unjust. God is essentially just and essentially against injustice. The very office of the God entails that He be essentially just. In view of the same, God has to reward the righteous people with paradisal bliss and punish vicious people by sending them to hellfire (Nadvi, 1983, p. 11).

Mu'tazilites believe that God has blessed man with the free will and liberty of action. He has been given the necessary power, therefore has to shoulder the requisite responsibility. According to Mu'tazilites, God is necessarily just in the light of the following verses of the Qur'ān:

1. Verily Allah will not deal unjustly with man in aught (*Al-Qur'ān*: 10:44).
2. And not one will thy Lord treat with injustice (Ibid, 18:49).
3. Allah is never unjust in the least degree (Ibid, 4:40).

In the light of the Qur'ānic world-view and value-system, the Mu'tazilites assume and appropriate a thoroughly teleological Cosmos or Order. The assumption and appropriation of such a Cosmos or Order, are born out of hundreds of explicit verses of the Qur'ān. To begin with, we have scores and scores of verses which bring out

God to be All-Just, All-Good, All-Wise and All-powerful. God has not created this Universe for the sake of fun. He is absolutely devoid of whimsicality and capriciousness. The Universe has been created by God with definite ends and purposes. The God of the Qur'ān is thoroughly teleological. The Universe we are living in is not an illusion, an imitation or a reflection, it is a real universe. God has created man and provided him guidance through revelations bestowed upon His Prophets from time to time. These revelations incorporate true beliefs and good values. The Cosmic Order is a Moral Order as well. There are objective values and purposes informing this Moral Order. The ultimate source of Moral Order is God Himself. God is obliged to always do the best (Eliade, 1987, p. 236).

> The justice of God "makes its necessary upon Him not do anything contrary to justice and equity. God's Wisdom always keeps in view what is salutary for His servants; therefore He cannot be cruel to them. He cannot bring into effect evil deeds. He cannot ask His servants to do that which is impossible (Sharif, P. 201).

God cannot impose impossible obligations on us. Such stance would be contrary to His justice. The Qur'ān underlines that the Lord of Universe is Just, Wise, and Merciful. In view of the Justice, Wisdom and Mercy God cannot issue impossible demands. In this regard the Qur'ān says: "On no soul doth Allah place a burden greater than it can bear. It gets every good that it earns" (*Al-Qur'ān:* 2:286).

God also cannot do anything which is purposeless. The following verses of the Qur'ān make the purposefulness of God's actions clear:

> Behold! In the creation of the heavens and the earth; in the alternation of the Night and the Day; in the sailing of the ships through the Ocean for the profit of mankind; in the rain which Allah sends down from the skies, and the life which He gives therewith to an earth that is dead; in the beasts of all kinds that He scatters through the earth; In the change of the winds, and the clouds which they trail like their slaves between the sky and the earth; (here) indeed are Signs for a people that are wise (Ibid, 2:164).

According to Mu'tazilites, good and evil are absolutely independent of God. He neither wants evil nor commands the acquisition of evil. Good and evil are created by human violations or exercise of freewill. Human beings are given necessary or requisite power to either carry out good actions or evil ones. Shahrastani brings out that Mu'tazilites are fully convinced that God is wise and just, and accordingly, evil and injustice cannot be attributed to Him. It is for His servants to either be obedient or commit sins, believe or disbelieve, do righteous or vicious deeds etc. It is human beings who commit good or bad actions and will definitely receive what is due to them in hereafter (Shahrastani, 1984, p. 44, Sharif, 2001, P. 205). God is perfectly wise and, according to Mu'tazilites is always rationally and purposefully directed in His specific motives. In keeping with His perfect knowledge, God chooses the best and most expedient means to carry out His acts (Muthhari, 2004, p. 13). The power given to man signifies choice, which choice in accordance with the principle of Divine justice (Bosworth, 1993, p. 790). It is perfectly in keeping with Divine justice that God most gracefully grants us the requisite power to carry out our duties. It is, furthermore, perfectly in accord with our rational and moral imperatives.

PREDESTINATION AND FREEWILL

God being necessarily just, necessitates that man be free; that he be the author of his own actions. It is the assumption of human freewill that implies human responsibility. This was precisely the contention of Qadarites and the Mu'tazilites espoused and underlined the significance of this contention with greater enthusiasm. Thus, they became true successors of Qadarites. The key contention of Mu'tazilites was that human freewill, human responsibility and reward and punishment for good or bad deeds necessarily imply each other. Without freewill, human beings cannot be held to be responsible for their good or bad actions and cannot be accorded reward for good deeds and punishment for bad ones. In view of the same, all the Mu'tazilites advocate that the man is the real author of his own actions (Sharif, 2001, p. 200).

In view of the fact that man is the author of his own deeds, it is necessary for God to reward him eschatological happiness and fulfillment. Shahrastani explained the same in the following words:

> The Mu'tazilah maintained that man has power over his good and bad deeds and is also their creator. Man, therefore, deserves reward or punishment in the next life for what he does in this one. One cannot ascribe to God evil and injustice or an act of unbelief and sin, because if he created injustice he would be unjust; likewise, if he created justice he would be just (Shahrastani, 1984, P. 42).

Mu'tazilites bring out that human beings create some acts by recourse to *Mubasharah* and some acts by way of *Taulid*. The term *'Taulid'* implies the necessary occurrence of another act from an act of the doer. It is through *'Mubasharah'* (social interaction) that man creates conditions for his guidance or misguidance. It is from the social interaction that conditions for his success or failure are created by way of *'Taulid'* or (consequences). God has nothing to do either with *Mubasharah* or with *Taulid*. He is not interested in who carries out in terms of righteous or vicious deeds. God has blessed man with freedom of will. It is for man either to carry out good deeds or bad ones as per his freewill. God through the Qur'ānic guidance and commandments asks us all to abide by the teachings of Islām and refrain from vicious deeds. It is for man to be an obedient Muslim or ignore the guidance offered in the Qur'ān and commit sins in the violation of all revelatory commandments. Human actions carried out of obedience or guidance of His commandments, are independent of God, are autonomous human actions. Mu'tazilites believe that man has been blessed with freewill and the necessary ability to be obedient to God or commit sins out of disregard for divine directives (Sharif, 2001, p.201).

The Mu'tazilites doctrine of freewill is derived from the following verses of the Qur'ān:

1. Every soul will be (held) in pledge for its deeds (*Al-Qur'ān:* 74:38).

2. Verily never will Allah change the condition of a people until they change it themselves (with their own souls) (Ibid, 13:11).

3. We showed him the Way: Whether he be grateful or ungrateful (rests on his will) (Ibid, 76:3).

4. Then shall anyone who has done an atom's weight of good, see it! (Ibid, 76:7).

5. And anyone who has done an atom's weight of evil, shall see it (Ibid, 76:8).

6. Whoever works righteousness benefits his own soul; whoever works evil, it is against his own soul (Ibid, 41:46).

7. Whatever good, (O man!) happens to thee, is from Allah; but whatever evil happens to thee, is from thy (own) soul (Ibid, 4:79).

8. If any do deeds of righteousness, --Be they male or female- -and they have faith, they will enter Heaven, and not the least injustice will be done to them (Ibid, 4:124).

THE ESSENTIALITY OF GOOD AND EVIL ACTIONS

For Mu'tazilites Good and Evil are innate in things themselves. The Divine prescriptions and proscriptions across the thirty Chapters of the Qur'ān are revealed in response to things and actions being innately or inherently good and bad (Sharif,

2001, p. 201). Mu'tazilites advocate that the differentiation between good and evil can be carried out by recourse to human reason; the job of revelation in this regard, is only confirmatory. Good and evil being essential and innate, are rationally driveable. We can understand the difference between good and evil actions in their essence. We do not need revelation to differentiate good action from bad ones (Mutahhari, 2004, p. 13).

Mu'tazilah point out that goodness, truth, beauty, and justice etc, are realities in themselves. Take for example, justice as it is reality in itself. As God is necessarily just in voice, He carries out acts in accordance with this standard of justice. Some acts are essentially just and some act essentially unjust. Actions are not just because they have been commanded by God; rather, they are commanded by God because they are just and other actions are prohibited by God because they are essentially or inherently unjust. If we reward doers of good actions, we are doing justice. Similarly, if we are not punishing the doers of evil, we are not being just. Acts of exploitation, oppression and cruelty are inherently unjust and therefore have been forbidden by God. As God is absolute in His Perfection, Wisdom, and Justice, He carries out actions that are accordance with the standard of justice (Sharif, 2001, p. 202). In view of the same, Mu'tazilah stress that we understand the significance of revelation, the necessity of faith in Allah and relevance of His commandments through Reason. In fact, it is Qur'ān which underlines the pre-eminence of reason as source of understanding what's good and what's evil. The Qur'ān repeatedly underscores that we should try to reflect, understand, listen, pounder over. It asks us to refrain from blindly following our ancestral beliefs and values. It underlines that we should adopt the right course of action through the application of Reason. Our Reason is sure guide to understanding and interpretation for the Qur'ān.

PROMISE OF REWARD AND THREAT OF PUNISHMENT

Mu'tazilites bring out that the Qur'ān features verses in which God promises to reward righteous believers and punish vicious believers as well as unbelievers. He is bound to fulfil His promise of reward and punishment. The believers, the sinners and the unbelievers will have to receive what they deserve in the life hereafter. Mu'tazilites underlined that an authentic faith in God and its verbal profession are not sufficient conditions of eligibility of admission to the sanctum sanctorum of Islām. In order to qualify as Muslim, we also need to avoid the major sins *(Kabair)*. The unrepentant Muslim sinners and unbelievers are bound to be condemned to the hellfire (Nadvi, 1983, p. 50). God cannot reward the evil doers or punish the righteous people. The natural and just course is that God must reward the righteous people and punish the sinners and unbelievers (Bosworth, 1993, VII, 790). Human beings, have to merit reward or punishment as per their conduct and behaviour. So, God must necessarily reward the virtuous and punish the vicious people. Of course, as brought out in the several verses of the Qur'ān, God can pardon anyone and punish anyone as mentioned in the Qur'ān:

> And remember We took a Covenant (to this effect): Shed no blood amongst you, nor turn out your own people from your homes: And this ye solemnly ratified, and to this ye can bear witness (*Al-Qur'ān:* 2:84).

However, the sinners and unbelievers will have to merit His pardon. They have to sincerely repent and seek forgiveness from God. Also, only those who have sincerely repented and sought pardon from Allah, will merit intercession of the prophet on the Day of Judgement. Only the acceptance of sincere repentance is obligatory on God (Bosworth, 1993, p. 124).

Several verses of the Qur'ān emphatically bring out that promise of the reward and punishment will be definitely fulfilled. Anyone who has done an atoms weight of good shall see and anyone one who has done an atoms weight of evil shall see. "Then shall anyone who has done an atom's weight of good, see it!" (*Al-Qur'ān:* 99:7). "And anyone who has done an atom's weight of evil, shall see it" (Ibid, 99:8).

Accordingly, the unbelievers and sinners will have to be sent to hellfire and righteous Muslims will have to join the paradisal realm. Each one of the authentic believers and sinners and unbelievers will find himself and herself either in the hell or in the paradise in face of what they earned here and now (Bosworth, 1993, p. 124). The promises of God are inviolate. The following verses of the Qur'ān bring out the same: "Never think that Allah would fail His apostles in His promise: For Allah is Exalted in Power, --the Lord of Retribution" (*Al-Qur'ān:* 14:47) "Verily, Allah will not fail in His promise" (Ibid, 13:31).

According to Mu'tazilites, the essential job of religion is to prepare or motivate human beings to command what is righteous and forbid what is vicious. All the Prophets were sent by Allah asking people to command what is right and not command what is wrong. From the Qur'ānic verses and teachings of the Prophet one gathers that commanding what's right or forbidding what's wrong is integral to Islām and essential for believers. According to the Qur'ān: "Let there arise out of you a band of people inviting to all that is good, enjoining what is right, and forbidding what is wrong: They are the ones to attain felicity" (Ibid, 3:104).

3.6 THE Ashairah

Ash'arites school of Muslim philosophical theology originated from the Mu'tazilah milieu of thought, understanding and interpretation. The founder of the school was Abu'l-Hasan al-Ash'arī $9^{th}/10^{th}$ century A.D. Muslim theologian and thinker, who started his carrier as a radical advocate of Mu'tazilite principles of philosophical theology or Kalām. Al-Ash'arī was suddenly inspired and activated to work out a critique against the basic principles underlined by Mu'tazilites. Consequently, he advanced an account of Muslim philosophical theology which was not only critical but also antithetical to the vision and mission of Mu'tazilites.

According to al-Ash'arī, the Ash'arites differed from Mu'tazilites on following counts:

1. Essence and Attributes of God.
2. Freedom of Will.
3. The Criterion of Truth.
4. The Standard of Good and Evil.
5. The Vision of God.
6. Createdness of the Qur'ān.
7. Divine Justice.
8. Promise of Reward and Threat of Punishment.
9. The Rational Basis of God's Actions.
10. God's Treatment of His Creatures (Sharif, 2001, P. 229).

We shall be providing an outline of Ash'arites tenets as they fundamentally impinge upon the question of justice.

Firstly, one of the most fundamental principles of Ash'arites philosophy, closely connected with the question of justice, is their perspective on the freedom of human will. The Ash'arites deemed themselves to be taking a middle path between radical predestinarianism advanced by Jabarites and radical libertarianism advanced by Qadarites and subsequently by Mu'tazilites (Sharif, 2001, p. 223) According to Ash'arites, the Orthodox people especially Jabarites hold that all human actions are predestined by God. Man is bereft of any power whatsoever to initiate any action. It is All Power-full God who does everything and man, on his own, can do nothing. All actions originated from God Who has absolute power over everything. As against Jabarites, the Mu'tazilites and Qadarites hold that man is granted with freewill, liberty of actions, and power and is fully responsible for all his actions, righteous and vicious.

As against Mu'tazilite emphasis on the reality of human choice, al- Ash'arī underlined on the Omnipotence of God. He insisted that everything good and evil is willed by God. They accepted the Mu'tazilite contention that the power of choice in human beings is created by God. However, they interpreted it to mean that man has been given the power to acquire actions. The original and effective power rests with God. They derived power from God. Power given to man is incapable of creating anything. According to al- Ash'arī "the true meaning of acquisition is the occurrence of a thing of event due derived power and it is an acquisition for the person by whose derived power it takes place" (*Al-Maqalat,* 190, pp. 539-540). God does create in man the power or the ability to undertake an action. God also grants to man the power to choose between what's right and wrong. However, man's free choice is too ineffective to produce an action. God creates the action corresponding to the power created by Him in man (Sharif, 2001, pp. 229-230). Man only intends to do an action. He acquires the merit or demerit of the action because of his intention to do a good or bad action. Shahrastani tries to explicate the Ash'arites standpoint in following words:

> God creates in man, power, ability, choice and will to perform an act, and, man, endowed with this derived power, chooses freely one of the alternatives and intends or wills to the action, and, corresponding to this intention, God creates and completes the action (Shahrastani, 1984, p. 53).

Another quotation from Shahrastani can furthermore illustrate the Ash'arite position:

> Man has power over his acts because he experiences in himself an obvious distinction between movements such as trembling and shaking and those which are voluntary. This difference is due to the fact that voluntary movements are brought into being through power, and as a result of the choice of the one possessing that power. On the basis of this Ash'arī says that the acquired act is the one possible through the power present, and the one that occurs under the created power. According to Ash'arī's principle, however, the created power has no effect on the bringing into being of an act, because from the point of view of coming into being there is nodifference between substance and accident (Ibid, pp. 81-82).

Ash'arites made a distinction between creation of an action and acquisition of an action or between *Khalaq*, and *Qasb*. While God is the creator *(Khaliq)* of human actions, man is just an acquisitor *(Muktasib)*. Man is not himself a creator of his actions. Creating a thing, an event or an action, is the sole prerogative of God. Ash'arites advanced a different interpretation of those verses of the Qur'ān which apparently accord freedom of will to human beings. Nadvi advanced the following words in outlining the contention of Ash'arites:

> The Qur'ān ascribes some actions to human energy, not in the sense that they really originate from it, but in the sense that their completion is partially due to it, it is owing to the power of appropriation which man exercise to complete his work that the Qur'ān rhetorically ascribes some actions to human ability (Nadvi, 1983, p. 67).

The Ash'arites based their standpoint on basis of those verses of Qur'ān which advocate absolute Divine Will and prearrangement of human actions. Some of the key contentions of Ash'arites, which impact their understanding and interpretation of justice, may be outlined as hereunder:

THE PROBLEM OF REASON AND REVELATION

There is a fundamental disagreement between Mu'tazilites and Ash'arites as to the primacy of Reason and Revelation. The Mu'tazilites prioritise Reason whereas the Ash'arites prioritise the Revelation. For Mu'tazilites, Reason is the basis of truth and Reality whereas for Ash'arites Revelation has a more fundamental role in appropriation of truth and reality (Sharif, 2001, pp. 230-231). In case, their crops up disagreement between Reason and Revelation, Ash'arites would go in for Revelation. While Mu'tazilites would offer unqualified obedience to Reason, Ash'arites would in the final analysis, surrender to Revelation. In fact, this is the key contention between the rationalist *Kalām* of Mu'tazilites and orthodox *Kalām* of Ash'arites. Ash'arites contend that the fundamental principles of Islām cannot be rationally verified, demonstrated or justified. We need to believe in those fundamental principles on the basis of Revelation. Of course, faith needs to be supported by sound rational consideration as well. However, Reason cannot be accepted as the basis of Islām or the basic source of Islām.

GOOD AND EVIL

The problem of Good and Evil is one of the central problems of Muslim theology. Mu'tazilites hold that it is through Reason that we can determine what's good and what's evil. As against Mu'tazilites, Ash'arites hold that revelation is the real criterion of good and evil. No action is good or evil in itself; it is the Revelation or Divine Law which categorizes actions to be either good or evil. It is Revelation which is the sole criterion of qualifying actions to be good or evil. Any action commanded by *Sharī'ah* is good and any action prohibited by *Sharī'ah* is evil.

THE PURPOSE OF DIVINE ACTS

According to Ash'arites, God is the only cause of things, persons, actions and events. Only He has the power to create actions or direct events. However, God's actions need not necessarily serve any end or purpose. God acts out of His infinite Wisdom. Such a Divine Wisdom is beyond the ken of human understanding. God does not follow any standard of wisdom. Whatever is done by God is full of wisdom. God is not bound by any teleological order. He is not bound to act in the best interests of His creatures. His actions are absolutely independent of any teleological considerations. He does whatever He likes to do. However, in the final analysis, His actions are full of wisdom for He is absolutely wise.

REWARD AND PUNISHMENT

According to Mu'tazilites, "God is bound to fulfil His promises of reward and punishment" (Sharif, 2001, p. 236). They insist that God has got to reward the virtuous and punish the vicious. In the light of promises made by God in the Qur'ān, He cannot punish the virtuous and reward the vicious. As against Mu'tazilites, Ash'arites hold that God is All Powerful and Absolutely Free. He is free to reward anyone and punish anyone. We cannot bind His Will to teleological considerations. In view of the fact that He is eternally Wise and Just, He does reward the virtuous and punish the vicious. However, in view of His Infinite Mercy, God can forgive any wrong doer. God according to the Qur'ān can forgive anyone and punish anyone. His Wisdom and Justice do not necessarily qualify His Mercy or His Omnipotence. They refer to the following verses in justification of their contention:

1. And God's ordering is in accordance with a fixed decree (*Al-Qur'ān:* 38:36).

2. Verily, God accomplishes what He ordains-He has established for everything a fixed decree (Ibid, 45:24).

3. God creates what He wills (Ibid, 3:65).

4. And you do not wish unless God wishes (Ibid, 85:20).

5. Say: All is from God. (Ibid, 4:78.).

6. And God gives means of subsistence to whom He will without measure (Ibid, 2:212)

7. And whatever is in the heavens and whatever is in the earth is Allah's, He forgives whom He wills and chastises whom He wills; and God is forgiving, Merciful (Ibid, 3:129).

8. No evil befalls on the earth nor in your own souls, but it is in a book before we bring it into existence, surely that is easy to God (Ibid, 57:22).

3.7 THE Shīah

Shi'ites like Mu'tazilites, underscore the fundamental significance of justice with reference to both God and people. They regard the Justice of God as one of the five principles of religion *(usul al-din).* Shi'ites like Mu'tazilites, emphasized on Divine Unity and Justice. They agreed with Mu'tazilite perspective on Divine Justice, Divine Wisdom, Human Freewill and Human Reason. However, despite the basic agreement with Mu'tazilites, Shi'ites also brought out considerable differences with them. For example, Shi'ites like Mu'tazilites do not deem freewill as an absolute delegation of authority and freedom amounting to curtailment of Divine Freedom and complete independence of human actions. The Shi'ites have tried to advance an intermediate position between Mu'tazilites and Ash'arites (Muthhari, 2004, pp. 20-21).

According to Shi'ites, Divine Justice, Human Reason and Freewill do not in any way qualify the principle of Divine Unity in essence or acts. They affirm Divine decree and destiny with respect to all Beings without qualifying Human freedom with respect to voluntary actions (Ibid). While for Ash'arites, all actions of human are created by God, for there is no creator except God. He does whatever He wants and He Judge as He pleases. Whatever He does is just (Nasr, & Leaman 1996, p. 131). For Mu'tazilites, Divine Justice necessitates that man should be the author of his actions. He should have complete freedom and should have no influence from outside. Such a claim denies the doctrine of the unity of creation (Sharif, 2001, p. 229). As against both Mu'tazilites and Ash'arites, the Shi'ites hold a midway between the two positions known as *al-amr-bayn al amrayn*. The Shi'ite position was defined by Imam Jafar Ibn Muhammad al-Sadiq (d.148/765). He defined Shi'ite position as neither predestination nor delegation but a position between the two (Al-Kulayani, 2002, pp. 222-224). Shī'ah thinkers have underlined that human beings have been given freedom to do or not to do various actions across spectrum. Therefore, they are fully responsible for what they do and what they do not. Accordingly, they will be proportionately rewarded or punished in the hereafter. Nevertheless, Shī'ah thinkers qualify their standpoint by positing a middle position; God has not predestined human beings to commit the sins and then destined them to be consumed in the hellfire. Nor has God delegated them with powers to operate in complete freedom. In such a case He would not have asked them to enjoin good and forbid evil. Human beings operate in between complete determinism and complete freedom of will. However, the Shi'ites also add that human actions are of our own making as we are given the capacity to do certain actions or avoid certain other actions. God asks His servants to carry out good deeds and refrain from committing misdeeds (Nasr, 2001, P. 133)

According to Imām Ali (A.S) the oneness of God signifies He is beyond the limitations of our understanding and the Justice of God means that He is innocent of any blame. (Nahj al Balaghah, saying, 462). According to Al-Muthhari, Hazrat Ali (A.S) defined justice as keeping everything in its own place and giving everyone his due (Muthhari, 1979, p. 8). He who finds it hard act justly should find it harder to deal with injustice (Nahj al Balaghah, sermon, 15). Hossein Nasr, a contemporary Iranian thinker migrated to America has tried to summarize the Shi'ite standpoint in the following words:

> The question of justice as espoused by Imāmates has remained untainted, respected, and original and without a blemish on the doctrine of unity of creation. Our actions have two dimensions. The first is commissioning the

action of our own volition. The second is the creation of that action by Allah's will with which He imbued us, giving us the power to commission the action. Imāmates Shī'ah Muslims adhere to all these matters. Therefore, they have made Divine Justice one of the five principles of religion (Nasr, 2001, pp. 134-135).

Shi'ites have extensively written on matters pertaining to Justice, predestination, delegation, freewill etc. Hundreds of treatises have been compiled on these questions. Al-Shaykh al-Mufid, Nasir al-Din al-Tusi, Allamah al Hilli and Sadr al-Din Shirazi can especially be cited as having written detailed commentaries on such philosophical and theological matters. We shall quote some lines from Shaykh al-Mufid by way of illustration:

> Allah is just, gracious. He created men to worship Him and forbade them to disobey Him. He did not charge anyone with any obligation beyond their ability. His creation is far from frivolity and His action is free from impropriety. He has remained above sharing His servants' actions and rose above coercing them to do any deed. He does not chastise anyone except when they have sinned and does not chide any bondsman or bondswoman except when they do a horrid deed. He does not do injustice, not even an atom's weight (Ibid, p. 130).

GOOD AND EVIL

For Ash'arites, Revelation is the real criterion of designating actions to be good or evil. Actions are not good or evil in themselves. It is Divine Law that defines them to be either good or evil. Reason only confirms what's given by Revelation. It is through Revelation that we can understand what's good and what's evil. As against Ash'arites, Mu'tazilites held that it is Reason rather than Revelation which is the criterion of determining some action to be good or evil. Actions are good or evil in their essence and we can rationally understand what's good and what's evil. The role of Reason is more fundamental than that of Revelation. What we can rationally appropriate is merely confirmed by Revelation.

Shi'ites or Imāmates are more akin to Mu'tazilites than Ash'arites in this regard. Shi'ites agreed with Mu'tazilites that actions are good and evil in their essence and we can understand their goodness or badness by recourse to Reason. We are intellectually capable of differentiating good actions from bad actions and Divine Law need not necessarily be deemed to be a precondition for understanding what's good and what's bad. They held that justice is a reality in itself and God being Just and Wise carries out acts in keeping with this standard of justice. Some actions are essentially just such as rewarding the doers of good. Some actions are essentially bad such as punishing the doers of good. Accordingly, God being absolutely Good, Perfect, and Just, He carries out acts that accord with such an objective standard of justice (Muthhari, 2004, pp. 8-9). Murtada Muthhari has clarified the Shī'ah standpoint in the following words:

> The principle of justice is the criterion of Islām, that is one has to evaluate all things in the light of this criterion. Justice belongs to the causes (or reasons) of religious laws and not one of the effects (or products) of the laws. What the faith prescribes is not just, but what justice demands is the faith (Muthhari, 2004, pp. 170-171).

The Qur'ān repeatedly underlines that God is Wise and His Wisdom necessarily entails that His actions are purposeful and He has not created this Universe in vain. The Wisdom of God implies He has created the best of all possible worlds (Muthhari, 2004, p. 62).

Another important thinker Allamah al-Hilli has brought out the following principles as postulates of His Wisdom and Justice:

1. He does not commit evil deeds.
2. He acts with purpose and wisdom and all His actions are proper.
3. He cherishes devotion and hates transgression.
4. He does not commission anyone with that which is beyond his ability.
5. He does not judge only that which is just, but all actions. Accordingly, His bondsmen should accept His judgment, bitter or sweet as the case may be. (Nasr, 2001, pp. 130-131).

REWARD AND PUNISHMENT

Mu'tazilites deemed human beings to be completely either doing good or evil and therefore, deserving reward or punishment in the next world. God cannot go against His promises and will definitely reward the virtuous and punish the vicious. Every good action is bound to follow by reward and every bad action is bound to follow by punishment. On the other hand, the Ash'arites held that there is nothing binding on God. It is not obligatory on God to reward the virtuous and punish the vicious. God is All Powerful and Absolutely free in His will, He can forgive whom He will and punish whom He will. Human beings will be rewarded with paradise or condemned to the hellfire not in accordance with their actions but by recourse to Divine Mercy.

The Shi'ites tried to appropriate mid way position between Mu'tazilites and Ash'arites. Hossein Nasr tries to Summarize Shi'ite position in the following words:

> God ought to carry out His promises, but He is not forced to do so. He should carry out His promises because this is in accordance with justice and fairness, and to go against such principles would be repugnant. Yet He does not have to act in accordance with those principles, in the sense that he is obliged in more than a moral sense to do so (Ibid, p. 124).

It is impossible to even conceive of God being unjust. It is impossible of human imagination to conceiving God not rewarding the virtuous and not punishing the vicious. Muthhari writes:

> Resurrection and the judgement of good and evil deeds, and rewarding good-doers and punishing evil doers are in themselves manifestations of Divine justice. One of the standard proofs presented for the validity of resurrection is that since God is all-wise and all just, He does not abandon human deeds without reckoning and reward or punishment (Muthhari, 2004, p. 201).

Hazrat Ali (A.S) brings out the following:

> It is possible God grants respite to the oppressor but He never abandons him without punishment; He awaits him on his path of crossing, and will block him much like a bone stuck in the throat (Najh al-Balaghah, sermon. 96).

DECREE (*QADA*) AND DESTINY (*QADAR*)

The Arabic word *Qada* means Decree and *Qadar* means Destiny. The word *qada* translated into English means 'to decide' 'to settle' or to 'to judge'. The word *Qadar* means 'to measure' or 'to determine'. Al-Muthhari explicates the distinction between *qada* and *qadar* in the following words:

> The events of the world are said to be divinely decided because they take place within the knowledge of God and are subject to His will. They are said to be divinely determined because their time, place and nature are determined in accordance with a system fixed by God (Muthhari, 2004, p. 39).

There are three views with regard to happening of events:

1. Firstly, there is a view that events have no relation to the past and in such a theory the very concept of 'destiny' is meaningless.

2. Secondly, there is view that every event has a cause, every effect has a cause; however every cause does not necessitate a particular effect or that any given

effect can emanate only from the particular cause. Such a theory can assume that the whole Universe has only one cause and agent and that is God. Everything and every event emanates directly from Him. All human actions as well directly emanate from the Will and Knowledge of God. No event can be brought about by ineffective human will and power. Such a view is Fatalism.

3. Thirdly, there is view that all the worldly events are governed by causes. There is an inevitable link between the events. Such an inevitable link between the events and causes signifies destiny.

Fatalists or Destinarians have advanced the famous argument concerning the knowledge of all things, no events can be said to be hidden from His knowledge, which is neither changeable nor violable. In view of the same, it can be safely assumed that every event must coercively and forcefully happen in keeping with Divine knowledge. For example, God has been eternally knowing that such a person would be committing such a sin at a particular time and place, that person is bound to commit that sin. He cannot do otherwise.

According to Shi'ites, such an argument is premised on a misunderstanding. It takes Divine knowledge and the system of causes and effects into account separately. The Fatalists presumed that Divine knowledge is attached to the occurrence and non-occurrence of events independently of the system of causation. Such a system is incontrollable. Therefore, we need somehow to curb the natural Laws and human freewill so that any inconsistency is not registered between Divine Eternal Knowledge and events of the world (Muthhari, pp. 84-85).

The Shi'ite thinkers argue that such a conception of Divine knowledge is completely wrong and premised on utter ignorance. The Eternal knowledge of God is not something separate from the system of causation. His knowledge is nothing but the knowledge of the system of causation itself. It is the present world with this very system that is necessitated by Divine knowledge. Divine knowledge has no attachment with the occurrence of an event. What knowledge of God necessitates is that the appearance of the effect should ensue from its particular cause. It places no role in the determining of free agent. The following words from Muthhari illustrate the same:

It must be remembered that while all things in this world and all system of causation are known to God, they at the same time constitute His knowledge also. This world and all its systems are Allah's knowledge as well as known to Him. This is because God's Essence Embraces the essence of every entity eternally and the essence of everything is present before Him. It is impossible for any entity throughout the universe to be hidden from Him. He is everywhere and with every entity (Ibid, pp. 86-88).

There are numerous verses of the Qur'ān which substantiate the validity or truth of decree and destiny. The Prophet is also reported to have said that Allah has determined it in advance as to who will go to paradise and who will go to hellfire. The Prophet, further, reported to have said:

> There is not a single soul without it being decreed by God for a place in either heaven or hell, and decreed to be either happy or unhappy. A man then retorted, "O Messenger of God! Are not we better off if we were to stick to our lot and forsake our work? The messenger of God replied. Nay, work. Everything is made easy. As for the happy ones, their course of action shall be facilitated towards the people of happiness. As regards the unhappy ones, their actions shall be within easy reach in the direction of wretchedness (Nasr, 2001, pp. 136-137).

Hazrat Ali (A.S) is reported to have admonished one of his companions in the following words:

> Woe to you! You take it as a final and unavoidable destiny according to which we are bound to act. If it were so there would have been no question of reward and punishment and there would have been no sense in God's promise and warnings. On the other hand, God, the Glorified, has ordered His servants to act by free will and has cautioned them against evil doing. He has placed easy obligations on them, not heavy ones. He gives them much reward in return for little action. He is disobeyed not because He is overpowered. He is obeyed but not under duress. He did not send Prophets just for pleasure (Nahj al-Balaghah, Sermon, 78).

REFERENCES

1. Eliade, M. (1987). *Encyclopedia of Religion.* Vol. VIII, New York: Macmillan.

2. Shahrastani, M. A. (1984). *Muslim Sects and Division.* Translated by. A. K. Kazi and J. G. Flynn, London: Boston, Melbourne and Henley.

3. Nasr, H. & Leaman, O. (1996). *History of Islamic Philosophy.* Vol. I, II, London: Rutledge.

4. Shushtery, A. M. A. (1938). *Outlines of Islamic Culture Philosophical and Theological Aspects.* Vol. II, Bangalore City: Bangalore Press.

5. Sharif, M. M. (2001). *A History of Muslim Philosophy.* Vol. I, Delhi: Adam Publishers and Distributors.

6. Bosworth, C. E. (1993). *Encyclopedia of Islam.* Vol. II, VII, New York: Leiden.

7. Parrott, J. (2017). *Reconciling the Divine Decree and Free Will in Islam.*

8. Nadvi, M. (1983). *Muslim Thought and its Source.* Delhi: Idarah-i-Adabiyat-I.

9. Donaldson, D. M. (1953). *Studies in Muslim Ethics.* London: S. P. C. K.

10. Ali, A. Y. (2007). *The Holy Quran.* New Delhi: Islamic Book Service.

11. Mutahhari, M. (2004). *Divine Justice.* Translated by Sulayman Hasan, Abidi, Murtada, Shuja-Ali Mirza, Qum: International Center for Islamic Studies.

12. Al-Ashari, A. H. (1930). *Maqalat al-Islamiyyinwalkhtilaf al-Musallyyin,* Vol. II, Istanbul.

13. Al-Kulyani, Y. (2002). *Usul al-kafi.* Vol. I. Tehran: Intisharat-e-Islami.

14. Hazrat Ali (AS). (2016). (2nd edition). *Nahj al Balaghah.* Abbas Book.

15. Mutahhari, M. (1979). *Bist Guftar.* Qum: Sadra.S.

CHAPTER-IV

CONCEPT OF JUSTICE IN MODERN MUSLIM THOUGHT

4.1 SHAH WALI ALLAH (1703-1762)

Shah Wali Allah was not a fully-fledged modernist thinker as was Sir Sayyed Ahmad Khan whom he greatly impacted in his religious, social, political and ethical thought. However, Shah Wali Allah's thought is definitely a turning point with reference to medieval Muslim or philosophical weltanschauung mainly consolidated by such jurisprudential luminaries as Imām Ahmad bin Hunbal, Imam Ibn Taymiyyah and Muhammad bin Abdul Wahhab. Shah Wali Allah's social, political and legal thought is definitely imbued with crucial and critical social scientific insights and elements of value.

For Shah Wali Allah, *'Adalah'* (Justice) is the most outstanding and distinctive characteristic of human society. Shah Wali Allah deems justice to be an essential moral quality of human beings. He underlines that such individual moral consciousness ought to be augmented on the social plane as well, for social institutions cannot operate in an atmosphere of moral degeneration. In fact Shah Wali Allah's conception of *'Adalah'* covers all human pursuits in their entirety and diversity. When we express *Adalah* in our mores, manners, eating and dressing habits it is called *Adab* (etiquette). When we maintain *Adalah* in matters pertaining to income and expenditure it is called 'economy' when we maintain *Adalah* in operation of the State it is called politics (Sharif, 1961, p. 1560)

For Shah Wali Allah, economic justice is the fundamental condition for the realization of the objective of justice at the social plane. No healthy and balanced development of society is possible without economic justice. Every social group has to have an economic system catering to the material requirements of every members of the society. Fulfilment of necessities or contingencies is essential for commitment to higher purposes of life. Without such commitment, they can actually turn neglectful of the eternal eschatological bliss.

Shah Wali Allah, as a social and political philosopher is firmly rooted in Islamic discourse. However, he is not merely guided by the textual sources of Islam; rather he offers considerations and arguments with a view to justifying the doctrinal, ethical and socio-political teachings of Islam. Historically speaking, like other religions, Islām also has esoteric, exoteric, nouminal and phenomenal, legal and spiritual dimensions or aspects. The Islāmic beliefs and values need to be spiritually realized as well as institutionally implemented. The beliefs and values of Islām are incorporated into the Qur'ān. However, their acceptance and allegiance as well as ethical, social and political implementation was carried out by the struggle of the Prophet and his Companions. The Prophet was a supremely successful spiritual teacher. However, he was also head of the State looking after the military, the judicial, the foreign and other executive affairs of the government. After the demise of the Prophet, Abu Bakar, Umar, Uthman and Ali served as his rightly-guided successors from 632 to 661 A.D. the State was committed to social, political, and economic Justice. Justifying the Islāmic State as well as its reestablishment in modern times, Shah Wali Allah advances the following words:

> it is the general authority to undertake the establishment of religion through the revival of religious sciences, the establishment of the pillars of Islām, the organisation of Jihad and its related functions of maintenance of armies, financing the soldiers, and allocation of their rightful portions from the spoils of war, administration of justice, enforcement of *hudud*, elimination of injustice, and enjoining good and forbidding evil, to be exercised on behalf of the Prophet (peace be upon him) (Al-Ghazali, 2004, p. 86).

Shah Wali Allah is possibly the greatest social, political and economic thinker of modern Islāmic period. He was an outstanding Ṣūfī of 18th century India. However, he did not teach Muslims to merely engross in their personal eschatological salvation through God-realisation. Spirituality is anchored on the fulfilment of both *Haququ'llah* (rights of God) and *Haququl ibad* (rights of human beings). A mature and authentic spiritual response cannot be just oriented to the rights of God and ignore the social, political and economic duties human beings have towards one another. We cannot be authentically spiritual in isolation from our social, political and economic responsibilities. Human beings can earn spiritual realization only through their social, political and economic engagements and commitments. Islām does not consider a human being as an isolated individual being but as a member of the community.

Taking a balanced view of an individual's relationship to society, Islām underlines the establishment of social justice to be a precondition for the development of the individual. Shah Wali Allah takes this question in great detail in his magnum opus Hujjat Allah al-Balighah. In this book, Shah Wali Allah takes up the question of human relationships entailing the necessity or inevitability of social, political and economic factors, conditions, institutions, values, laws, guidances etc. According to Shah Wali Allah, it is human requirements, needs, wants and desires which orientate or urge him to action. In view of the fact that all human requirements, needs, wants, and desires cannot be met by each individual by himself, we need a social organization or setup carrying out collective ventures and undertakings to meet out the requirements of the entire population to the maximum possible extent. The first and foremost need of the society is to ensure individual and collective security, safety and peace. In keeping with the requirements of security, safety and peace, human beings join hands to form the government. Accordingly, when they join hands to satisfy their material needs they establish economic system. In order to regulate social, political and economic institutions as well as interpersonal relationships, human beings have to design awesome moral value systems and legal codes of conduct. A balanced social system creates the most conducive environment for our spiritual growth and cultivation of inner peace.

Shah Wali Allah underlined that the role of the State cannot be just confined to providing of safety and security of the individuals. The State has the responsibility to strive for the happiness and progress of society as a whole. The State has the responsibility of eradicating such evils as bribery, usury, adultery, gambling etc. It should regulate the trade and commerce and see to it that malpractices are eliminated. One crucial responsibility of the State is to channelize the energies of the people in different occupations. For example, there should be a proper distribution of people in such fields of operation as agriculture, commerce, army etc. The State should devise a sound economic system which can lead to social justice, leading to the happiness of society. In case a State fails to establish social justice, its downfall becomes unavoidable. The following words from Shah Wali Allah indicate the social and political orientation of his thought:

> After a careful analysis I have come to the conclusion that there are two main factors responsible for the decline of the Muslim culture. Firstly, many people have abandoned their own occupations and have become parasites on the government. They are a great burden on the public exchequer. Some of these are soldiers; some claim themselves to be men of great learning and, thus deem it their birthright to get regular financial

help from the State. There are not a few who get regular donations, gifts, and rewards from the Court as a matter of past custom, such as, for example, poets and clowns. Many of the people belonging to these groups do not contribute anything to the welfare of society, yet they are allowed to stick its blood. The sooner the State gets rid of these parasites, the better. Secondly, the government has levied an exorbitant rate of tax on the agriculturists, cultivators, and traders. Added to this is the cruel treatment meted out to the tax-payers by officials at the time of collecting the taxes. The people groan under the heavy weight of taxes while their economic position deteriorates at an alarming speed. This is how the country has come to ruin (Sharif, 1961, pp. 1563-1564).

Shah Wali Allah does not agree with those who advance the view that poverty is loved by God and it is not becoming of a Muslim to strive for social justice and economic welfare. For Shah Wali Allah, such an interpretation of Islām is patently erroneous. Islām does teach voluntary contentment but does not ask us wallow into penuriousness or abject poverty. Islāmic teachings are oriented to social justice and welfare. The forced poverty upon certain classes or sections of society is totally unaccepted to Islām. Shah Wali Writes:

> The forced starvation of certain classes is highly detrimental to the welfare of society. It is not a virtue but a crime. Islām grants no licence to any class to compel others to as hewers of wood and drawers of waters. It aims at the achievement of social justice, which is possible only when society is free from class conflict and everyone is provided with an opportunity to develop his latent powers and capacities and strengthen his individuality through free and active participation in the benefits of his material and cultural environment.... Islām teaches that this strong concentrated individuality, sharpened and steeled through a life of active experience, should not become obsessed with self-aggrandizement; it should be devoted to the service of God and through this to the good of mankind. Islām never preaches its followers to submit themselves ungrudgingly to an eulogized by the Holy Prophet-justice which not only safeguards an individual against an attitude of arrogance and self-conceit, but develops in him a power to spurn the temptations, bribes and snares with which an unscrupulous ruling clique tries cynically to corrupt the integrity and character of the subjects (Ibid, p. 1562).

According to Shah Wali Allah, the State has the responsibility to promote the good life of its citizens. If it does so, it is the duty of its members to be loyal to such a State. However, if the State operates in violation of all norms of propriety, then it is the duty of its members to strive to overthrow it and replace it with a better system of governance. Abdul Hamid Siddiqi brings out the following in this regard:

> For him the State is a means to an end and not an end-in-itself. Therefore, he holds that the possession of coercive power cannot be defended

> regardless of the ends to which it is devoted. If a State wields this power honestly, then the highest duty of an individual is to become a loyal member of that State, but if it is a State only in name and is in reality a blind brute force, then it becomes the bounden duty of its members to overthrow it. Thus an important duty of an individual is to become a member of the State, but more important than this is his duty to judge the quality of the State of Which he is member (Ibid).

The question of social justice cannot be fully appreciated unless we understand the complexities of human psychology as they have worked out the concrete historical evolution of man. Shah Wali Allah warns: "Remember that sensual qualities selfishness, greed etc, develop in unbalanced personalities. The abundance of riches brings these brutal qualities into action" (Sharif, p. 1567).

When we cultivate love of worldly riches, our will to power and distinction is further enhanced. An aristocrat not only wants to be born to appropriate riches, they also want others to live in abject poverty. Such a social, political and economic psychology leads to division of society into haves and have not. Thus, haves or aristocrats have treasures at their disposal; they command the economy and control social, political and economic affairs. On the other hand, disappropriated masses are condemned to survive with extraordinary struggle. Such a social condition leads to callousness of the rich who watch tyranny and oppression with complete indifference. Religious people concentrate on their personal salvation in the midst of such a scenario. Consequently, we have indescribable suffering and unacceptable oppression, leading to complete collapse of social, political, economic and moral order. In order to substantiate, his contention, Shah Wali Allah, by way of example, advances an explanation of the rise and fall of Roman and Persian civilization, in the following words:

> The historical records eloquently speak of the fact that the Romans and the Persians held sceptre and crown for a fairly long. According to their own cultural requirements, they added a good deal to the luxuries of their age. Their highest aim was to lead a life of pleasure.... The people who could make their lives more luxuries flocked from all the corners of the world in order to achieve this objective. The aristocracy having thus become immersed in the pursuit of pleasures, there began a race amongst its members to excel one another in this respect, and matters became so bad that a rich who tied a belt around his waist costing less than one thousand gold coins was looked down upon by others. Everyone tried to possess a magnificent palace with a number of orchards attached to it. Their whole life came to be centred upon sumptuous foods, gaudy and attractive dresses, horses of the finest stock, coaches and carriages, and a

retinue of servants.... They got used to all forms of luxurious living, and this was in fact the canker eating into the very vitals of their society (Ibid, pp. 1567-1568).

This meant a heavy drain on the purse of the people, as the kings and rulers were forced to levy an exorbitant rate of taxation upon the artisans and cultivators. The poor had perforce to raise a banner of revolt against the ruling clique. But under the circumstances this was well-nigh impossible; therefore, the only course left for the poor was to live as bond slaves and lead their lives like donkeys.... In short, the lower strata of society were so much occupied in the service of the aristocracy that they found no time to pay any heed to the problems of the life hereafter (Ibid, p. 1568).

However, Shah Wali Allah was not against leading a happy life but what he underlined was that unbridled pursuit of worldly riches is not conducive to the development of a just and egalitarian social order. Muslims should cultivate necessary detachment to worldly pleasures in order to sustain their civilization on an equitable basis.

4.2 JAMAL AL-DIN AL-AFGHANI (1898-1897)

Jamal al-Din al-Afghani was nineteenth century Islāmic scholar, intellectual, thinker and revolutionary. He was deeply concerned about prevailing injustice across Islāmic lands. He travelled across Islāmic lands and found that Muslim masses were facing widespread injustices at hands of their rulers. Muslim rulers were themselves being directly or indirectly driven by European powers which further aggravated the social, political and economic problems of the people. Afghani wanted Muslims rulers to put an end to foreign domination. In order to achieve such an objective, Muslim rulers lead it to carry out internal reforms in the countries. They also needed to co-operate among themselves with a view to reducing the foreign domination to the least. Accordingly, Afghani proposed that Muslim rulers should grant their subjects the right of participation in the exercise of authority. The subjects should be allowed to elect their assemblies so that they can discuss affairs in keeping with the principle of consultation (*Al-Qur'ān:* 27:32). Afghani also wanted Muslim rulers to put up a Pan-Islāmic front against foreign domination. Such a Pan- Islāmic Movement to go a long way in minimizing the foreign domination of Muslim lands. Afghani was of the opinion that only in societies governed by higher spiritual religions, can man hope to finds some justice and happiness (Khadduri, 1984, p. 198). It is religion which urges every man to achieve perfection and prepare for the eternal life. In such a struggle for perfection man is asked to abstain from evil and wickedness which can lead oppression and injustice. He is also asked to appropriate such virtues as righteousness and justice. He is asked to cultivate the virtue of *Al-Haya* which restrains him from committing acts of shamefulness. Such a virtue is more important than law for the upkeep of justice, peace and order. Nextly, the virtue of trust also provides the ground for honest dealing between man and man. Similarly, the virtue of telling truth is essential for social relationships. It is on such virtues that the standard of order and justice can be founded. In the absence of such virtues human beings will be consigned to domination and oppression.

4.3 ABUL A'LA Maūdudī (1903-1979)

Abul Ala Maūdudī was a twentieth century exponent or advocate of Islāmic State. He was categorically convinced that only an Islāmic State can provide solution to the social, political and economic questions faced by mankind. An Islāmic State is distinct from ancient emperorships and monarchies as well as modern secular democratic republics in so for as it accepts God to be the locus of Sovereignty. In ancient authoritarian regime, it was King or the Emperor who was deemed to be the locus of sovereignty. In modern secular democratic republics, sovereignty is supposed to be vested with the people of a given country. As against such ancient and modern regimes, an Islāmic State is anchored on the Sovereignty of Allah. It is God who is the only Sovereign in the world and it is godliness which is the only standard of distinction and honour in an Islāmic State. Human beings cannot be said to be having any superiority or incurring any inferiority on the basis of caste, creed, color, culture, language, ethnicity, nationality etc. People who are pious and God-fearing are honorable in the eyes of God. In view of same, our economic, political, social, intellectual and cultural institutions need to be run on the guidelines provided by faith in the Sovereignty of Allah. These institutions need to be presided over by persons of moral and spiritual eminence, people who have soaked themselves into godliness. No institutions, programmes, activity, strategy, policy etc that does not accord with injunctions of Allah can be deemed to be justified in the Islāmic State. All programmes of action and policies of implementation need to be carried out in spirit of godliness; otherwise they would be deemed to be lacking in legitimacy and unjustifiable. Sovereignty of Allah should be the basis of the State. No other basis of State can protect human values, human rights or social, political and economic justice.

The theories of State or Sovereignty as advanced by such political thinkers as Bodin, Hobbes, Locke, Rousseau and Austin etc. are not acceptable to Maūdudī. In his writings, Maūdudī has advanced plausible arguments undermining the ideological assumptions of western theories of State and Sovereignty. Such Western theories or ideologies as nationalism, secularism, contractualism, humanism etc. cut religion off from social, political, economic and cultural concerns and problems. For example, throughout history, political opportunists have exploited and enslaved people in the name of nationalism. They dominate social, political and economic conditions of numberless generations of people under the pretext of nationalism. The emergence of Nation-States in modern Europe has posed fresh social, political and economic challenges to the modern man. According to the modern nationalists, people belonging to the various races, tribes, languages, cultures and religions can together operate as members of a Nation-State. People of these diverse identities can together work for the cultural, educational, economic, political, and social development of the nation.

For Maūdudī, the political ideology of nationalism deems advancement of the rational interest to be the foremost aim of a Nation-State. In view of the same, various nations are pitted against one another and powerful nations exploit weaker nations both economically and politically. Therefore, nationalist competition can never lead to global peace and justice (Maududi, 1959, p. 8).

Modern Nation-States have also accepted 'Secularism' as an important ideological guideline. Secularism assumes that 'State' has no religion. In fact, the State just cannot have any connection with religion. A State has to provide civil supplies, educational opportunities, transport facilities, medical facilities, jobs, drinking water, electricity etc to all the citizens without any regard to religion. Religious beliefs and injunctions are beyond to the secular responsibility of the State. In a democratic, liberal and secular society, all people have freedom of conscience and they can choose to be either religious or non-religious in the light of their preferences, choices, and institutions. However, Maūdudī maintains that a secular State and society can never do justice or achieve equality, for they are neutral or indifferent to Divine commandments. In contrast to a secular State, an Islāmic State is guided by religious faith and therefore oriented to peace and equality.

Similarly an Islāmic State does not entirely agree with democracy. While a democratic government is based on the principle of the sovereignty of the people, Islāmic State is based on Sovereignty of Allah. Nevertheless, Maūdudī underlines that there is a fundamental agreement between some crucial Islāmic values and democratic values. While democracy stands for human equality and equal human rights, the original manifesto of Islam is equality and equal human rights as well. Islām does not entertain any discrimination on grounds of caste, color, creed or class. The Prophet of Islām emphasized that no one is superior to anyone else except on grounds of piety and godliness. An Arab has no superiority over non-Arab, neither is a non-Arab superior to an Arab. A white man is not superior to a black man, nor is a black man superior to a white man. Only the most pious people are the most superior people. All human beings have descended from Adam who was made of clay. No person or group of persons will suffer in an Islāmic society on account of circumstantial disadvantages. Thus, on certain crucial values, there is perfect equanimity between Islām and democracy.

Islām is also in complete agreement with democracy on human rights. God has given human beings freedom of speech, freedom of thought and freedom of conscience. No human being or groups of human beings are entitled to establish dictatorship on any other person or groups of persons. The human rights of any person are inviolate in an Islāmic society. Each person can choose any profession, follow any religion or follow the dictates of his own conscience. The head of an Islāmic State is entitled to enforce whatever has been underlined in the Qur'ān. However, he cannot enforce on his own sweet will. The head of an Islāmic State and his advisors or ministers can be elected through popular mandate. However, in the name of justice and equality, Islām cannot promise to establish a classless society. An Islāmic State can claim to provide equality of opportunities to all its citizens. It cannot commit itself to establishing a social order where every citizen will be equally intelligent or talented. One of the vital differences between Islām and democracy is that Islām cannot accept the principle of majority vote under all circumstances. Islām exhorts each one of us to cooperate with what is righteous and not cooperate with what is vicious. We cannot assume that majority will always be on the side of righteousness or minority votes will always be supporting what is morally unworthy. Under given circumstances one single individual can be voting for what is righteous and the rest of them can support what is explicitly immoral or even illegal. In view of the same, we cannot expect Islām to be imposing tyranny by majority. Thus, Maūdudī finds important similarities between Islām and democracy. However, there are vital differences between the two systems as well (Maududi, 2011, pp. 32-37).

Maulana Maūdudī is critique of contemporary western political ideologies such as nationalism, secularism, democracy and both socialism and capitalism, for he is convinced that all these ideological programmes cannot deliver justice to mankind at large. It is so because these ideologies are Allah-independent and *Dīn* -independent. For Maūdudī, only those saturated with piety, godliness and faith in the eschatological accountability, are eligible for holding political, legal, economic, managerial and administrative offices. Any head of the State, Caliph, Imām or *Ameer* or any minister, judicial officer, administrative officer or any other functionary must believe in the Sovereignty of Allah, exercise His authority in subordination to and in accordance with the laws prescribed in the Qur'ān. All the functionaries of State are to be governed by the *Sharī'ah* as embodied in the Qur'ān and authentic practices and traditions of the Prophet. The government has to be carried out in accordance with *Sharī'ah* and everyone from the office assistants to the head of the State will have to operate within the prescriptions of *Sharī'ah*. It is the collective duty of the Islāmic community to see to it that righteous actions are carried out and vicious actions are proscribed. Only such an Islāmic Order can establish a just and egalitarian social order. Islām is a complete code of conduct and capable of guiding in every department of life. Allah has sent His Prophets from time to time to guide mankind. However, they were everywhere opposed by elites and the ruling cliques. However, people at large accepted the message of the Prophets and believed God to be Creator of the world. However, belief in the existence God as Creator of the world was not enough. God had to be accepted as Nourisher *(Rab)* and Lord *(Ilahi)* of the universe as well. When we believe in His Lordship, it means we have to completely surrender our entire lives to Him and carry out His Orders with devotion and in unqualified subordination. Belief in God as only Nourisher of the universe signifies that we expect everything from Him; whether happiness, profit, power, honor, or pain, loss, dishonor etc. However, wealthy and powerful people were not prepared to live their lives in complete subordination to Allah. Rather they wanted to Lord over the common masses themselves. Maūdudī writes:

> The desire for godhood can take place only in the head of man. It is only man's excessive lust for power and desire for exploitation that prompts him impose himself on the other people as a God and compel their obedience, force them to bow down before him in reverential awe and make them instruments for his self-aggrandizement. The pleasure of posing as a God is more delicious than anything that man has yet been able to discover. Whoever is possessed of strength of wealth, cleverness or farsightedness or any other superiority develops a strong inclination to out step his natural and proper limits to extend his fellow men as are comparatively feeble, poor, weak minded or deficient in other respects (Ibid, pp. 10-11).

Historically speaking, most of the Kings and Emperors did not reject God as Creator of the universe. However, for all practical purpose, they refused to believe in the lordship of Allah. They refused to accept that all human beings should be only committed to Allah and carry out only His orders. The Kings and Monarchs rather treated their subjects as slaves or servants. They treated them in most inhuman ways. Besides Kings and Monarchs, Popes in Europe, Brahmins in India, Muslim spiritualists in various countries, twentieth century Communist party Lords in Soviet Union in China, Fascists in Italy and Nazi leaders of Germany etc. can be cited as other examples who Lorded over thousand of millions of people at various points of history.

The upshot of Maūdudī's political thought is that justice and equality are impossible of attainment in societies and States run by so-called western democrats, secularists, and nationalists or their eastern counterparts. The root cause of injustice, inequality, exploitation and enslavement is the presence of so-called nationalist secular democrats across the globe and the absence of Islāmic States based on the Sovereignty of Allah. Mankind needs to be educated on these lines for the restoration of justice, equality and peace in the world. Maūdudī writes:

> It should also be brought home, to man that in the whole of this universe there is only one Sovereign, Master and Ruler. No one else is entitled here to issue his commands nor does, in point of fact, anyone else's writ run here. Therefore, he should not agree to become the instrument of any Will other than His Will nor accept the command of any other, nor bow down before anyone else. There is no one worthy to be styled in this world as His Majesty because all majesty resides in Him. There is no one here who can be called His Holiness, because all holiness is vested in Him. There is no being to be styled as His Highness, because highness is the sole attribute of God. There is no one here fit to be called His Lordship for lordship belongs to God wholly and solely. There is no legislator here and no law-giver, for the only law deserving obedience is the Law of God. There is no one here besides Him, who can rightfully

claim to control and regulate the affairs of humanity, none who can administer justice in his own right, none who can answer the prayers of man and from whom man can expect help or succor in his distress; there is none besides Him, who possesses the keys of authority and there is nobody else who can claim absolute and unconditional allegiance for human beings. All men are but servants and there is only one Master. Hence it behooves us to deny obedience to all authority which itself does not owe allegiance to Him and to refuse to serve any person or group of persons who act independently of the Will and purpose of the Creator. This is the root and foundation of all reformation. On this foundation alone the whole superstructure of individual character and social organization can be planned anew after pulling down the old structure, and all the problems of human life that have arisen in the past or will arise in future can be solved in a new manner (Maududi, 1959, pp. 25-27).

4.4 SAYYED QUTB (1906-1966)

Sayyed Qutb was a twentieth century Egyptian scholar of Islāmic studies who advanced an interpretation of or perspective on Islām akin to the vision and mission espoused by Maulana Abul A'la Maūdudī of Indian subcontinent during the very same twentieth century. For Sayyed Qutb, as against Modern West, Islām is not overly analytical and methodological and rather underlines a holistic or integrated vision of cosmos, man, and his social, political, economic, intellectual, cultural and artistic questions. The following words by Sayyed Qutb illustrate the same contention;

> Islām has one universal theory which covers the universe and life and humanity, a theory in which are integrated all the different questions; in this Islām sums up all its beliefs, its laws and statutes, and its modes of worship and of work. So the best method of studying Islām is to start by understanding its universal theory before going on to study its views on politics or economics or the relationship between communities and individuals (Qutb, 1953, p. 17).

Modern Western theories and even Judaism and Christianity have advanced philosophical perspectives or intellectual narratives which are oblivious to the need for a holistic vision. Such philosophical or intellectual perspectives and narratives may be deemed or described to be *Jahiliyya* (ignorance of the Divine Laws). Sayyed Qutb believed that the Qur'ān is a divinely promulgated constitution with a view to regulating all human actions in all possible situations. According to the Qur'ān, Islām signifies submission to the *Sharī'ah* and rejection of all other Laws (Qutb, 1999, p. 164).

Sayyed exhorts Muslims of the world to go in for an appropriation of an authentic philosophy of Islam. Fārābī, Ibn Sīnā, Ibn Rushd and many more are not authentic representatives of Muslim philosophy, they represent the Greek philosophy of Plato and Aristotle more than the philosophy outlined or underlined in thousands of verses of the thirty chapters comprising the Qur'ān. The sources of Muslim Philosophy are the Qur'ān, the *Sunnah* and the Traditions of the Prophet. Sayyed Qutb writes;

> The true Muslim Philosophy is not to be sought in Ibn Sīnā or Ibn Rushd, or such men as these who alone are known as the Muslim Philosophers; for the philosophy which they teach is no more than a shadow of the Greek Philosophy, and has no relation to the true Islāmic philosophy. The faith of Islām has a native universal philosophy, which must be sought only in its own familiar authorities: the Qur'ān and the Traditions, the life of its Prophet and his every-day customs. These are the authorities in which the student must study to find the universal Islāmic theory from which come all the Muslim teaching and laws, its modes of worship and of work (Qutb, 1953, p. 18).

For Sayyed Qutb, Islām put maximum emphasis on cultivation and execution of Social justice. However, Islāmic advocacy of justice is all-inclusive or all-embracing. justice, in the Islāmic context is not just social or distributive; material or economic, for Islām caters to the wholesale development of man, taking care of his physical, intellectual and spiritual sides (Ibid, p. 29).

According to Sayyed Qutb, Social justice cannot be achieved on a lasting basis, unless the society as a whole is infused with highest possible levels of conviction, conscience and spirituality. A spiritually educated society normally flowers into a just society. The establishment of social justice must become an imperative of our conscience. Merely legal and statutory promulgations cannot guarantee justice. Accordingly, Islām to begin with lays maximum emphasis on the conscientization of human society. Only a conscientized society or spiritually advanced society can provide a permanent basis for social justice.

Furthermore, Islām advances an integrated view of social justice. For example, Christianity advanced that we cannot attune ourselves to the Lord's kingdom of heaven unless we give up our attachment to the life of this world. We cannot achieve spiritual happiness unless we give up our physical pleasures (Ibid, p. 31). While such an assessment of Christianity can be assumed to be true, it is not the whole truth. The Christians underline on the spiritual needs of life. It is not always mature way of dealing with human condition to over emphasise our spiritual needs and to ignore our material requirements. The Communists on the other hand, do just the opposite. They emphasise that economic freedom alone can lead to happiness and justice. Man violates such values as justice and equality under the heavy burden of economic pressures. Sayyed Qutb agrees with the partial truth of this as well. However, he criticizes communism for ignoring the spiritual needs of life.

As against Christianity and communism etc, Islām take cares of all sides of life. According to Islām, we cannot separate spiritual desires of man from his bodily appetites or his moral needs from his material needs. Qutb writes;

> When the conscience is freed from the instinct of servitude to and worship of any of the servants of Allah; When it is filled with the knowledge that it can of itself gain complete access to Allah; then it cannot be disturbed by any feeling of fear of life, or fear of its livelihood, or fear for its station. This fear is an ignoble instinct which lowers the individual's estimation of himself, which often makes him accept submission. But Islām insists strongly that glory and honor are the rights of man, and insists on the guarantee of an absolute social justice, under which man shall not suffer from neglect (Ibid, p. 35).

The Qur'ānic emphasis on human equality is, according to Sayyed Qutb, the bedrock of a social justice. Islām does not discriminate between human beings on ground of caste, creed and colour nor does it accord any superiority to any social, racial, linguistic, cultural group. Human equality extends beyond patriotism and religion. The believers and unbelievers are equal in origin and they have been created from the same male and the same female i.e. Adam and Eve (Ibid, pp. 47-48). The Qur'ān says:

> O mankind! Reverence your Guardian- Lord, who created you from a single Person, created, of like nature, his mate, and from them twain scattered (like seeds) countless men and women (*Al-Qur'ān*: 4:1).

To begin with, there was one soul; from it came its mate; and from the two of them there spread both men and women. So, all are brothers and sisters. The following verses of the Qur'ān testify to the same:

> O mankind! We created you from a single (pair) of a male and a female, and made you into nations and tribes, that ye may know each other (not that ye may despise each other). Verily the most honored of you in the sight of Allah is (he who is) the most righteous of you (Ibid, 49:13).

Sayyed Qutb advances another quotation as follows:

> These races and tribes, were not made for the purpose of rivalry or enmity, but for that of mutual knowledge and friendliness; all of them in

the eyes of Allah are equal, and there can be no superiority except in piety. But this is another question, unconnected with origin and nature; in these respects, "People are all equal as the teeth of a comb," as says the noble Prophet of Islam (Qutb, 1953, p. 47).

The Qur'ān emphasises on human equality in several of its verses:

> If any do deeds of righteousness, --Be they male or female- -and they have faith, they will enter Heaven, and not the least injustice will be done to them (*Al-Qur'ān*: 4:124).

> Whoever works righteousness, man or woman, and has Faith, verily, to him will We give a new Life, a life that is good and pure, and We will bestow on such their reward according to the best of their actions (Ibid, 16:97).

> And their Lord hath accepted of them, and answered them: Never will I suffer to be lost the work of any of you, be he male or female: Ye are members, one of another (Ibid, 3:195).

Sayyed Qutb emphasises that Islām upholds human, social and spiritual equality. In fact it is passionately concerned about human equality. It accords complete and universal equality. It transcends all racial and national considerations. The social or human equality taught by Islām cannot reduce just to economic equality, somewhat excessively underlined by Modern Western social, political and economic thinkers.

Sayyed Qutb emphasises on mutual responsibility enjoined by Islām. In fact mutual responsibility is one of the foundations of social justice in Islām. Sayyed Qutb writes:

> Islām lays down the principle of mutual responsibility in all its various shapes and forms. In it we find the responsibilities which exist between a man and his soul, between a man and his immediate family, between the individual and society, between one community and other communities, and between one nation and the various other nations (Qutb, 1953, p. 55).

The following Quotation from Sayyed Qutb also deserves our attention:

> Islām grants individual freedom in the most perfect form, and human equality in the most exacting sense, but it does not leave these two things uncontrolled; society has its interests, human nature has its claims, but a value attaches also to the lofty aims of religion. So Islām sets the principle of individual responsibility over against that of individual freedom; and beside them both it sets the principle of social responsibility, which makes demands alike on the individual and on society. This is what we call mutual responsibility in society (Ibid).

According to Sayyed Qutb, man has certain responsibility towards himself as well. He must control himself from being driven by desires. He must purify his appetites. He must pursue righteousness leading to salvation. The Qur'ān underlines that people who lead presumptuous lives and hankered after material pleasures of the world will find themselves in hell and those who restrain themselves from desires out of the fear of Allah will join the paradise (Ibid). Each human being is responsible as to what he does to his soul good or evil, benefit or harm. Each one is responsible for his or her worldly success or failure or eschatological reward or punishment. This is what is underlined by the following verses of the Qur'ān:

> Every soul will be (held) in pledge for its deeds (*Al-Qur'ān:* 74:38).

> He, then, that receives guidance benefits his own soul: But he that strays injures his own soul. Nor art thou set over them to dispose of their affairs (Ibid, 39:41).

Sayyed Qutb brings out that Islam enjoins mutual responsibilities between individual and his immediate family. The individual is based on the family and family is the basis of the society. It is through family and societal life that we can understand the significance of moral values and also appreciate the necessity of material requirements. Sayyed Qutb writes:

> We must think also of the responsibility which the individual has to society, and of that which society has to the individual. On each of these two Islam lays responsibilities, and for each of them it defines the limits to which he may go. In dealing with these responsibilities Islam tries as far as possible to harmonize their interests, and to remedy or to punish any loss which either of them may suffer in undertaking the duties which attach the various fields of life, spiritual and material (Qutb, 1953, p. 61).

Sayyed Qutb brings out that Islām enjoins on each individual to do his works conscientiously. Every individual also charged with the care of society. An individual is a watchman over a society. Each individual should shoulder the responsibility for the safety of society. Each individual is also charged with the duty of putting an end to any evil doing. The Qur'ān asks the believers to command what is good and prevent people from doing what is evil. The prophet has asked believers to prevent people from evil doing. The believers must root out the evil by their hands. In case they cannot do so they must propagate against evil doing. Lastly if such a propagation also not possible they must hate evil in their hearts. However such a stand indicates faith at its lowest. The societies are also responsible for care of its weak members. It must strive for their welfare and protect them. It must also fight in defence of its weak members (Ibid, p. 64).

> And why should ye not fight in the cause of Allah and of those who, being weak, are ill-treated (and oppressed)? --Men, women, and children, whose cry is: "Our Lord! Rescue us from this town, whose people are oppressors; and raise for us from Thee one who will protect; and raise for us from Thee one who will help! (*Al-Qur'ān:* 4:75).

The following words from Sayyed Qutb are worth quoting:

> Islām legislates for mutual responsibility in society in all shapes and forms; these forms take their rise from the basic principle that there is an all embracing identity of purpose between the individual and society. So Islām lays down a complete liberty for the individual, within limits which will not injure him and will not favour society at his expense. It safeguards the rights of society, and at the same time specifies its responsibilities on the other side of the balance. On these three foundations, then, an absolute freedom of conscience, a complete equality of all mankind, and a permanent mutual responsibility in society, social justice is built up, and human justice is ensured (Qutb, 1953 p. 68).

The Qur'ān lays unqualified emphasis on Justice:

1. Allah commands justice (*Al-Qur'ān:* 16:90).
2. And when ye judge between man and man, that ye judge with justice (Ibid, 4:58).
3. Whenever ye speak, speak justly, even if a near relative is concerned (Ibid, 6:152).

The followings words from Sayyed Qutb indicate the level of emphasis placed by Islām on execution of justice:

> This refers to that impartial justice which is absolute, and which cannot be swayed by affection or by hatred; the bases of this justice cannot be affected by love or by enmity. Such justice is not influenced by any relationship between individuals, or by any hatred between peoples. It is enjoyed by all the individual members of a Muslim community, without discrimination arising from descent or rank, wealth or influence. In the same way, such a justice is enjoyed by other peoples, even though there may be hatred between them and the Muslims. This is a high level or equity, to which no international law has so far achieved, nor any domestic law either (Qutb, 1953, pp. 93-94).

According to Sayyed Qutb, the basis of Islāmic polity is that rulers should be just, the ruled should be obedient and there should be collaboration between the rulers and the ruled. The Qur'ān explicitly asks the believers to "obey the Apostle, and those charged with authority among you" (*Al-Qur'ān*: 4:59). The Muslims need to obey the ruler only if his rule is in accordance with the injunctions of God and the teachings of the Prophet. If the rulers depart from the Laws prescribed by Allah or teachings of the Prophet, he is no longer entitled to the obedience.

Another feature of Islāmic politics is the collaboration between ruler and the ruled. The Qur'ān asks the believers to engage in mutual consultation. The Prophet used to consult his companions in matters pertaining to secular matters as conduct of war, daily administration, agriculture etc. So in light of the Qur'ān and teachings of the prophet the rulers and the ruled have to engage in consultation and collaboration with a view to maximize justice and minimize cruelty. Under no circumstances, the rulers cannot oppress the souls or the bodies of believers, infringe upon their sanctities or touch their wealth. The rulers just uphold the Laws of religion and preside over the observance of religious duties. Sayyid Qutb writes:

> It is the responsibility of the ruler to put an end to anything which occasion's hardship in the community, no matter what it may be; it is similarly his duty to encourage anything which is of any kind of profit to the community. But at all times he must be careful not to depart from the ordinances of Islām (Qutb, 1953, p. 98).

Sayyed Qutb brings out that Islām lays utmost emphasis upon individual welfare as well as societal welfare. Under no circumstances should the welfare of an individual or a society be jeopardised. Islām ensures individual as well as connective welfare by recourse to legislation and exhortation. It legislates with a view to maintaining a healthy society, capable of growth and improvement. It also exhorts people to raise their level up above their instinctual responses. Both legislative measure and exhortative proposal or recommendations aim at gradual up gradation of human life. Islām wants both individual and collective lives to arrive at maximum possible ideal or perfect levels (Ibid).

Islām commands its believers to pay the Holy tax *(Zakat)*. Such a payment is compulsory or mandatory. The ruler can use force against his subject if they withhold the taxes. Apart from holy tax *(Zakat)* Islām also allows a ruler the right to exact additional taxes with a view to preventing hardship doing away with penury and preserving the well being of the Muslim community (Ibid, pp. 100-101). However, it is through exhortation that Islām recommends the people to spend all their money in the way of God.

According to Sayyed Qutb, Islām aims at higher social justice then the mere economic justice. Such an elevated system of justice can only partially be worked out by recourse to legislative measures. Of course, Islām does establish a comprehensive system of Laws for the achievement of justice. However, on a higher spiritual plane, it makes conscience the basis of all executive, legislative and judicial measures. Conscience plays a pivotal role in the delivery of Justice. Sayyed Qutb writes:

> Islām places a great deal of reliance on the human conscience when it is educated; it sets it up as the guardian of the legal processes, to see that they are observed and maintained, and for the observance of the major part of the laws conscience alone is accountable. The giving of evidence, for example, is s fundamental matter which must be governed by laws, yet which, at the same time, must ensure the rights of men (Ibid, p. 71).

While human conscience is central to the execution and delivery of justice and carrying out of legal and human responsibilities, Islām also sets the fear of God as a sanction on the conscience. The human conscience is always under the omniscience of Allah. The Qur'ān maintains that:

> There is not a secret consultation between three, but He makes the fourth among them, --nor between five but He makes the sixth, --nor between fewer nor more, but He is in their midst, wheresoever they be: In the end will He tell them the truth of their conduct, on the Day of Judgment. For Allah has full knowledge of all things (*Al-Qur'ān*: 58:7).

The role of conscience is, nevertheless, absolutely crucial. The believers have to pay *Zakat* compulsorily but they can spend their entire lives and entire properties with a view to achieving eschatological salvation. Belief in afterlife and eschatological justice is integrally connected with the establishment of justice in the world. Faith in Allah, faith in the authenticity of Prophethood and faith in afterlife are unconditional postulates of morality in Islām, according to Sayyed Qutb.

4.5 MURTADA MUTAHHARI (1919-1979)

Murtada Mutahhari has dealt with the Question of justice in his two Books known as *'Adl-e Ilahi (Divine Justice) and Barrasi Ijmali Mahani-yiIqtisad-e Islami (A Brief Study of the Foundations of Islamic Economics).* He advanced a detail discussion with regard to justice in his first chapter of *Adl-e Ilahi (Divine Justice).* The discussion is carried out with reference to Mu'tazilite and Ash rite *Kalām*. In his book *'A Brief study of the Foundations of Islamic Economics'* Mutahhari explicates the concept of Social justice in the context of Islāmic discourse. The principle of justice has played a crucial role in the development of Muslim social philosophy. Mutahhari brings out the significance of the issue of social justice in the following lines:

> Firstly, I would begin with discussing the issue of justice in order to explain the effect of justice upon the principle of social justice; secondly, the denial of the principle of justice and its negative effect more or less in our thought was the main course of decline of social justice in Islām which could have been developed and based on scientific and rational grounds and could have become a guiding principle in jurisprudence. Consequently a kind of jurisprudence emerged which is now inconsistent with the rest of the principles of Islām and has no secure basis for social philosophy. If there would have remained freedom of thought (in Islāmic world) and the traditionalists *(Ahhab-e Sunnah)* would not have had dominance over the Champions of justice *(Ahl-e Adl)*, and if Shī'ahs also had not been trapped in the bit fall of *Akhbarigari*) then we could have had a codified social philosophy and our Jurisprudence also could have been based upon it and we had not been plunged into contradictions and dead ends (Mutahhari, 1403H, p. 170).

Nevertheless, in his book *'Ashnai ba Ulum-e Islami (An Introduction to the Islamic Sciences)'* Mutahhari has underlined that all Islām Schools of Thought have accepted justice as one of the Divine attributes. They have, of course, differed with one another about the interpretation of justice. For example, the Mu'tazilites believe that some actions are intrinsically just and some other actions are essentially unjust. Rewarding the virtuous and punishing the vicious is essentially just and God, accordingly, He has to reward the virtuous and punish the vicious. God cannot do otherwise, i.e. punish the virtuous and reward the vicious; for rewarding the vicious and punishing the virtuous is intrinsically unjust and we cannot even conceive God being unjust in any manner. Similarly, God cannot create human being to devoid of any power or capability of being virtuous, compel them to carry out sinful acts and then punish them. Creating such condition or doing such actions would constitute gross injustice. And, in no way, can God be said to be doing any injustice to his servants (Mutahhari, 1985, p. 63).

As against Mu'tazilites, the Ash'arites do not accept any action to be essentially or intrinsically to be just or unjust. God has not to do justice or carried out injustice. Whatever he does is justice. Incase God chooses to reward the sinners and punish the virtuous, it would still be justice. The Divine Will and Divine Actions are the sole determinants of justice.

Mutahhari brings out that Divine justice is one of the five essential doctrines of Shī'ah faith. It means that God is essentially just. Divine justice necessitates that man should be free and capable of acting according to his free will. Alternatively, man cannot be held to be responsible for his virtues and vices and cannot be rewarded and punished. Reward and punishment without capability and responsibility entails Divine injustice and such a possibility strikes at the very roots of Islamic world-view and value-system.

Mutahhari emphasized that Islām is a teleological world-view and believes in rights and universal justice, which are inherent in the very laws of nature. The fact that the universe we are living in is governed by natural laws, indicates its purposive and purposeful character. It signifies that the universe is definitely oriented to end or goal and that end or goal is established by its Creator, Allah. Islām according to Mutahhari, believes that every person born in this world has a right over the world. Corresponding to their natural rights they have obligations to fulfill as well. The following verses of the Qur'ān are cited by Mutahhari, in support of his contention:

1. It is He Who hath created for you all things that are on earth (Al-Qur'ān: 2:29).

2. It is He Who has spread out the earth for (His) creatures (Ibid, 55:10).

3. It is We Who have placed you with authority on earth, and provided you therein with means for the fulfillment of your life: Small are the thanks that ye give (Ibid, 7:10).

4. We have honored the sons of Adam; provided them with transport on land and sea; given them for sustenance things good and pure; and conferred on them special favors, above a great part of Our Creation (Ibid, 17:70).

Social philosophers do and can debate on precedence of rights and justice or vice versa. Mutahhari on his part underlines that justice precedes human rights. In fact, justice is the foundation of human rights. However, according to Mutahhari, human freedom and equality are not our rights; they are rather the source of human rights (Mutahhari, 1403H, p. 165).

With regard to the relationship between religion and justice, there are numerous accounts advanced by social philosophers and philosophers of religions. Different schools of *Kalām* have also carried out their interpretations with reference to this question. For example, Mu'tazilites advocate that justice is the criterion of religion which means that religion is constituted on the basis of justice. Ash'arites on the other hand, believe that what religion says is justice. Mutahhari, in holding justice is the criterion of religion, sides with Mu'tazilites. The following words from Mutahhari explicate his point of view:

> The principle of justice is the criterion of Islām, that is one has to evaluate all things in the light of this criterion. Justice belongs to the causes (or reasons) of religious and not one of the effects (or products) of the laws. What the faith prescribes is not just, but what justice demands is the faith (Ibid, pp. 170-171).

Mutahhari's view brings out that justice provides ground for the faith. It also indicates that justice is prior to faith. Such a view also indicates that justice is the criterion of good and evil. It further means that good and evil are rationally determined.

In view of the same, Mutahhari underlines that we should strive for the establishment of justice in numerous fields of human operation, for justice constitutes the locus standi as well as the raison d'être of religion. For Mutahhari, there is no contradiction between individual and social justice. We need to ensure social justice by respecting all the natural rights of human beings. Justice demands that right to life, right to freedom and right to equality must be upheld under all circumstances. For Mutahhari, natural rights are Divine origin. As against capitalism and socialism, Mutahhari advocates that only Islām can ensure social justice, for it guarantees natural rights to be of Divine origin.

Mutahhari underlines that the problem of justice and injustice intimately linked to the problem of good and evil. He tries to offer a kind of explanation and justification of phenomenon of evil. Moreover, he holds that the essence of evil is non-existence. Every evil is of the form of non-existence and non-being. And evil is an evil is because it itself non-being, deficiency and emptiness. Mutahhari makes it clear that evil is not a form of being, but is the form of emptiness and non-being.

Mutahhari maintains that evil is relative. He quotes Rūmī according to whom snake poison is not bad for the snake, it is bad for human beings and other animals. Snake poison is life to the snake, but it is death in relation to man. Hence there is no absolute evil in the world; evil is relative (Mutahhari, 2004, pp. 136- 137). Hafiz Shirazi also supports the interdependence of good and evil when he says: "In this garden nobody plucked a rose without thorn." "So the light of Mustafa is combined with the darkness of bolahab" (Ibid, p. 146).

Mutahhari argues that the system known as the universe cannot sustain itself without all of its dimensions. There have got to be lows and highs, valleys and mountains, darkness and lights, pains and pleasures, success and failures etc (Ibid). According to Mutahhari evil is essential to the appropriation of what's good. Similarly, ugliness is essential to the appropriation and appreciation of beauty. Ugliness and beauty are interdependent in the world (Ibid, p. 147).

While discussing justice Mutahhari takes up the problems of reward and punishment in the life hereafter. As perfect justice cannot be possibly established in life, God reward our good deeds in the life hereafter. So, He also punishes us for our vicious deeds in the hereafter as well.

Mutahhari has critically evaluated the capitalistic, liberalistic and socialistic system of governance. He thinks that capitalists and liberalists system of governance do not bother about social justice. On the other hand, the socialists are concerned about individual freedom and human rights.

4.6 ALI SHARIATI (1933-1977)

Ali Shariati was an eminent 20th century Persian scholar, Islāmist and sociologist, for whom Islām was a unique synthesis of moderate beliefs and values. Islām is neither overly philosophical, mystical or spiritual nor overly materialistic or technological. Islām is a delightful amalgamation of faith, idealism and spirituality. It is a dynamic way of life deeply and powerfully empowered by the spirit of equality and justice. The problem of justice constitutes the nuclear core of Ali Shariati's thought. The fundamental concerns of Ali Shariati are justice, politics and the true government (Marami, 1999, p. 132). The problem of justice is the kernel of his social thought and he has repeatedly underlined the significance of justice, especially with reference to Islāmic world-view and value-system (Zakaryyai, 1995, p. 73).

For Shariati, justice is one of the basic characterizing features of Islām and especially its Shī'ah version (Marami, 1999, p. 133). In his numerous writings, Ali Shariati appeals to the people to appreciate the value and significance of justice in the context of an authentic Islāmic society. He is critical of overly philosophical and theological interpretations of Islām. For Shariati, the problem of justice is not to be treated in terms of abstract bombast or jargon; it is rather to be treated as concrete social problem. He sees in Islām particularly Shī'ism the root of justice deep in society (Ibid, pp. 133-134). Having absorbed the elements Marxian philosophy and sociology, Ali Shariati considers the Islām to be the quintessential expression of a polarized view of society based on the struggling classes. The struggle should culminate into the societal transformation of the present class and political structures. The struggle should lead to a revolution in which the economic, political and social power of oppressed and dispossessed *(Mustadhafian)* is imposed over the proprietors and oppressors *(Mustakbirin)*.

Ali Shariati holds that justice cannot be explained merely on the basis logical and intellectual arguments. We cannot understand justice also on grounds of social expediency. We can understand justice with reference to order of the universe. If we maintain that the order of the universe is established on the basis of justice, we can conclude that our social system which is integral to social order should also be based on justice. For Shariati, justice signifies social equality, economic equality, and equality of human rights. The social and economic justice is premised on the unity of God and just universal order. Ali Shariati claims that his philosophy of Islām or interpretation of Islām is basically premised on the doctrine of unity of God. Ali Shariati says: "My world-view consists of *Tawhi*d. *Tawhid* in the sense of oneness of God is of course accepted by all monotheists" (Shariati, 2015, p. 82).

If we accept *Tawhid* and appreciate the real meaning of the world-view of *Tawhid*, we shall find that there is no contradiction in all of existence. There is no contradiction between man and nature. There is no contradiction between spirit and body. There is no contradiction between the world and hereafter. The world-view of *Tawhid* cannot accept even the contradictions based on economic, territorial, national, racial, political, social, class or legal grounds (Ibid, p. 86). Shariati criticized Karl Marx for deeming economic factor to be the basis of society. For Marx, moral, political factors and even human rights are of secondary significance. Justice also becomes secondary in the value system of Marx. For Ali Shariati the basis of society is the unity of God. Justice is an implication of unity of God (Marami, 1999, pp. 141-142).

According to Ali Shariati, an ideal Islāmic society is designated as *Ummah*, a word which implies progressive spirit and dynamic ideological vision:

> The word *Umma* derives from the root *amm,* which has the sense of path and intention. The nation *(umma)* is, therefore, a society in which a number of individuals, possessing a common faith and goal, come together in harmony with the intention of advancing and moving toward their common goal (Shariati, 1983, pp. 40-42).

An Islāmic *Ummah* is not premised on unity of blood or soil or shared material prosperity. *Ummah* signifies intellectual responsibility and common commitment to a common goal. The guiding principles of Islāmic society are equity and justice. Islām lays greatest emphasis on human equality and brotherhood. An Islāmic society is not driven by democracy or liberalism. It is not driven by aristocracy, dictatorship or oligarchy. Islām lays emphasis on unalloyed commitment and revolutionary leadership with view to achieving social progress and realizing the Divine destiny of man. This is what is signified by Imamate as well (Shariati, 2015, pp. 119-120). An Imamate signifies a political system in which each one is equal before law, in which each enjoys economic-equality, racial-equality and social and political freedom. The fundamental objective of an Imamate is to direct Islāmic society on the rules and criteria prescribed by the Qur'ān. However, in the process of historical evolution, an Islāmic society can appropriate elements of value from any quarter and reject elements disvalue from any quarter. While Ali Shariati appreciates the egalitarian spirit and ethos of socialism, he rejects class based ideology of capitalism. Capitalism promotes social, economic and legal discriminations.

Ali Shariati is considerably impacted by Marxian dialectics and philosophy of history. Transposing the Marxian dialects into Islāmic discourse, Shariati deems Abel and Cain-two sons of Adam-as two forces of historical dialectic. Shariati deems Abel to be representing the classical or primitive communism or the pastoral economy whereas the Cain representing the agricultural economy of private ownership. Abel was killed by the Cain and the history of war confrontation, opposition and contradiction begins. It sets the stage for a struggle between the ruler and the ruled. Ali Shariati writes:

> Abel the pastoralist was killed by Cain the landowner; the period of common ownership of the sources of production - the age of pastoralism, hunting and fishing- the spirit of brotherhood and true faith, came to an end and was replaced by the age of agriculture and the establishment of

the system of private ownership, together with religious trickery and transgression against the rights of others, Abel disappeared, and Cain came to the forefront of history, and there he still lives (Shariati, 2015, pp. 51-52).

According to Ali Shariati, the agricultural system restricted the sources of production in nature. Prior to agricultural economy, the individual did not exist in human society; it was the tribe all along. With the emergence of agricultural economy new values and priorities emerged as well. The unitary society in which all men were like the brothers in a single house was divided. The human family characterized by freedom, peace and tranquillity was divided into warring camps (Shariati, 2015, pp. 100-101).

Abel and Cain symbolize the ongoing confrontation between forces of faith, peace and self-sacrifice and the forces of passion, transgression and fratricide (Ibid, p. 102). Ali Shariati summarizes the dialectic of history in the following words:

> It is for this reason that the war of religion against religion has also been a constant of human history. On the one hand is the religion of shirk, of assigning partners to God, a religion that furnishes the justification for shirk in society and class discrimination. On the other hand is the religion of *Tawhid*, of the oneness of God, which furnishes the justification for the unity of all classes and races. The trans-historical struggle between Abel and Cain is also the struggle between *Tawhid* and shirk, between justice and human unity on the one hand, and social and racial discrimination on the other (Ibid, pp. 108-109).

Following the Qur'ānic Ali Shariati makes a distinction between the equity *(Qist)* and Justice *(Adl)*. Broadly speaking, these two concepts are used interchangeably. However Ali Shariati finds equity to be more important than justice. Ali Shariati writes:

> Justice *(adl)* refers mostly to the legal relations between individuals and groups, on the basis of the laws laid down in society. Equity *(qist)* refers to the equal enjoyment by all men of the fruits of their labour and of their rights, whether or not this is recognized by law. Justice implies the existence of a judicial system, and equity relates to the structure of society. In order to have justice, the judiciary must be reformed; in order to have equity, the social system must be changed-not superficially, but in its fundamental structure (Shariati, 2015, p. 109; Majmua-e- Asaar, 1983, pp. 36-39).

The following words bring out the distinction between justice and equity more explicitly:

> Justice means giving everyone his due before law. Equity *(Qist)* means giving every one according to his actual contribution, to the society. The concept of justice does not include the concept of equity *(Qist)* but the concept of equity includes it therein (Shariati, 1983, p. 39).

Islām is against all forms of injustice and inequality. Equality, brotherhood and justice are the cardinal values in Islām. One of the glorious achievements of Islām is the successful repudiation and rejection of racial inequality. The Blacks of Africa were powerfully gravitated towards Islām because of its espousal of racial equality. It was because of Islām's unqualified commitment to racial equality and justice that large number of Africans accepted the theological doctrines of Islām such as Unity of God, Authenticity of Prophet and Belief in Hereafter.

The Qur'ān has categorically asked Muslims to establish the award of equity *(Qist)*. The Prophet, the Islām and the community-all are asked and exhorted to establish an equitable social order, Muslims need to bring about an economic transformation and distributive revolution.

'Justice' is the cynosure of Ali Shariati's social and political philosophy. It is rather the ultimate legitimating criterion of politics and governance. It is only the realization of justice and equality to the maximum possible extent that a given political under or government can be legitimised. In view of the same, justice is the central or characterizing feature of Ali Shariati's social and political thought. He has mainly concentrated his attention on class struggle, social justice and human equality. Any political system bereft of human equality and social justice can be deemed and described as soulless system. Ali Shariati is firmly convinced that justice is the foundation upon which the whole universe is anchored. A just social system entails both Divine teachings and spiritual values as well as human rights and racial equality.

Ali Shariati's social philosophy is based on Islāmic world-view and value-system. However, he is deeply impacted by social philosophy of nineteenth and twentieth century. He is a democrat and an indefatigable advocate of freedom. He makes justice the centre point of his socio-political philosophy because he is convinced that freedom without justice does not amount to anything substantial. Justice is a precondition or prerequisite of an open and free society. For Ali Shariati, justice and freedom are not mutually exclusive but interdependent.

REFERENCES

1. Sharif, M. M. (1961). *A History of Muslim Philosophy.* Vol. II, New Delhi: Adam Publishers and Distributors.

2. Al-Ghazali M. (2004). *The Socio-Political Thought of Shah Wali Allah.* New Delhi: Adam Publisher and distributors.

3. Ali, A. Y. (2007). *The Holy Quran.* New Delhi: Islamic Book Service.

4. Khadduri, M. (1984). *The Islamic Conception of Justice.* Baltimore and London: The Johns Hopkins University Press.

5. Maududi, A. A. (1959). *Process of Islamic Revolution.* New Delhi: Markazi Maktaba Islami.

6. Maududi, A. A. (2011). *Political Theory of Islam.* New Delhi: Markazi Maktaba Islami.

7. Qutb, S. (1953). *Social Justice in Islam.* Translated by John B. Hardie, American Council of Learned Societies, Washington, D. C.

8. Qutb, S. (1999). *Charaggi Bar Faraz-e-Rah.* Translated in Iran: Qum Bija, Hamr, Bita.

9. Mutahhari, M. (1403 H). *Barrasi-ye Ijmali- ye Mabani-ye Iqtisad-e Islami, (A Brief Study of the Foundation of Islamic Economic).* Tehran: Hikmat Publication.

10. Mutahhari, M. (1985). *Fundamental of Islamic Thought.* Translated by R. Cambell, California: Mizan Press.

11. Mutahhari, M. (2004). *Divine Justice.* Translated by Sulayman Hasan Abidi, Murtada Alidina. Shuja Ali Mirza, Qum, International Centre for Islamic Studies.

12. Marami, A. R. (1999). *Barrasi-e-Muqay-e-Sei-e-Mafhoom-e-Adalat.* Tehran: Inqilab-e-Islami.

13. Zakaryyai, M. A. (1995). *Safar-e-Sabz.* Tehran: Ilhaam.

14. Shariati, A. (2012). (1st edition). *On the Sociology of Islam*. Translated by Hamid Algar, New Delhi: Iran Culture House.

15. Shariati, A. (1983). *Majmua-e-Asaar*. Vol. VII, XX, XXI, Tehran: Nilofar.

CHAPTER – V

CONCLUSION

The question of justice has had a perennial relevance. Man has been conscious of the problem of justice or the fact of injustice since times immemorial. Even when theoretical reflections upon the problem of justice were not advanced or clearly spelt out, the ancient man was terribly caught into deterministic and predestinarian attitudes. In view of the inscrutable twists and turns of life, the ancient man came to believe that everything was already fixed or decided upon by the Divine powers that be and man could not do anything about it. He willingly or unwillingly surrendered to the dictates of the faith. The gods had already dictated the minutest details about our lives and what has reached us could not have missed us and what has missed us could not have reached us. The Kings or Rulers were divinely ordained and it was in the fitness of things to submit to their dictates without any ifs and buts. If everything is already decided and if it has to happen come what may, hell or high water, then the question of justice could have arisen in the minds of ancient men.

Classical man was conscious of the problem of justice. Greek philosophers such as Socrates, Plato and Aristotle were first ethical and political philosophers concerned with the cultivation of virtues befitting an excellent person. A person in order to be just needed to be in-perfect accord with requirements of his duty. An Individual needed to perform his duties as determined by the Law, social customs and prevalent mode of thought. Plato prescribed the duties of different citizens and required them to develop corresponding virtues. Plato would advise a soldier that in order to be just he ought to be a brave man. He would advise a man in subordinate position that in order to be just he needed to accept authority and be self-controlled. For Plato, it is virtues which signify justice. Each virtue is a particular manifestation of the spirit of justice.

According to Plato, various types or classes of citizens are capable of performing different duties. They must perform their duties well. Such performance would be instrumental in building up a just social order. A harmonious and just social order can be achieved only if individual men and the larger society are guided by reason. In an Ideal State the rulers would be a class of philosopher-kings who are the embodiment of rationality and wisdom. The warriors who are courageous people would be assigned the duty of defending the State from external aggression and internal rebellion. The class of producers and distributors such as agriculturists, traders etc, characterized by self-control and temperance, would carry out multifarious economic and commercial operations.

According to Aristotle, human beings within any social order will have to deal with three types of justice: (i) Distributive Justice (ii) Retributive Justice (also defined as Remedial, Corrective or Rectificatory Justice) and (iii) Commutative Justice.

Distributive justice is the concern of the legislator. It deals with the allocation of honors and wealth. The fundamental principle of distributive justice is treating equals equally and unequals unequally. Retributive justice is concerned with imposition of punishment and payment of damages. It is the job of the judge to impose full restoration of any laws violated by any member of the society. Thirdly, the commutative justice should also be the concern of the judge. It deals with exchange of services and goods or transactions of buying and selling or letting and hiring. In this context, the judge should be guided by the principle of full equivalence.

Contemporary man is also active with the question of justice. Feminist thinkers in recent times have launched Movements and advanced discourses contending that women have been deprived of honor, equality and justice because of the prevalence of patriarchal institutions across history throughout the globe. Feminist thinkers try to advance historical, sociological and philosophical critiques of the patriarchal practices, institutions and modes of thought. They also analyze the conditions of women, the causes of their sufferings and the modes of their deprivation. The purpose of the feminist Movements and their discourses is to remove discrimination against women. Feminists strive for equal social, political, economic and cultural rights for women. They are committed to the provision of equal opportunities for women in all the spheres of human endeavor. Feminist argue that women suffer from various types of injustice and measures should be taken to restore justice to women.

Feminists bring out that there is large discrimination between men and women in the allocation of benefits and burdens. There is no appreciation of the contributions made by women for the sustenance of the society. The contribution of women to economic life is also not appreciated. There is no recognition for the unpaid work women do for the sustenance of the family and the community. There is no recognition of their child-bearing and child-rearing services. Women engage in cooking, house-keeping, cleaning, sewing, embroidery, etc. Such services are never taken into account. Thus, women make significant contribution to family income. Their significant contribution is characterized as unpaid and they are stigmatized as dependent on men. Furthermore, women also suffer from cultural climate of masculine dominance. Women experience shame, embarrassment and vulnerability in such an atmosphere. Thus, women experience discrimination in political, economic and cultural spheres of operation. Justice demands that such conditions be dismantled. Women need to be provided safety in their professional lives. They need to get better educational and career development opportunities. Women also need to get better professional training. Furthermore, their full contribution to national economic needs to be adequately factored into any balanced and responsible rational survey of income and expenditure.

There is also what's termed as subaltern perspective on justice. Such a perspective is deeply concerned with the discrimination of those sections of society who are permanently condemned to subordinate position. In view of the various inherent constraints in the social structure, certain sections of the society are continuously exploited, oppressed and marginalized. While the elite or the dominant class or the ruling class corners lion's share of all benefits, majority of the people comprised of subordinate groups are left with a meager share. Various subaltern groups suffer discrimination on grounds of culture, language, religion, region, race, caste, location, class, gender etc. These subaltern groups are systematically exploited and deprived of their rights. In order to restore justice to these groups, we need to protect their rights and appreciate their contribution to society. The subalterns should be given equitable share of social benefits, with a view to restoring their dignity.

Marxism seeks to grasp the questions of human society by recourse to historical analysis. Its fundamental assumption is that history is process of conflict between antagonistic classes. This conflict originates from the faultlines in the very mode of production wherein one class happens to be owning and controlling the means of production and dictates to the other class the terms and conditions of work, remuneration or daily wages. Such a conflict becomes impossible of resolution in the capitalist phase of history. At this stage, the only solution is to overthrow capitalism through a revolution. In such a revolution, all means of production such as lands, buildings, mines, forests, machinery, capital etc. would be placed under social ownership and control. In fact, the state comes into existence by recourse to class war, one class owning the means of production and other being forced to eke out its existence by share labor. It is the institution of private property which divides the society into haves and have-nots. The class owning the means of production dictates terms in all spheres of human operation. In order to protect its interests, the dominant class invents the state as the embodiment of political power. The dominant class imposes the state from above to serve its economic interests. The state has come into being at a particular stage of historical development. Thus, state is a means of class exploitation or an embodiment of social injustice.

Marxism pines for the emancipation of mankind from the capitalism to a classless and stateless society. Historically speaking, the state has changed from slave-owning feudal State and from feudal State to capitalist State. However, historical forces have not been able to transform the class character of the State itself. Such a transformation is to be accomplished by recourse to socialist revolution through which the proletariat (workers) would expropriate the bourgeois (capitalists). Capitalist system is inherently unjust and such an injustice can be removed by replacing the capitalist system by the socialists system. The socialist is brought about a proletarian revolution. In the socialist system all means of exploitation are abolished. The socialist system established after a revolutionary overthrow of the capitalist system. In the final analysis, a classless society will come into existence. It will be a society in which ownership of private property is abolished, for it is a source of exploitation and injustice. The abolished of private property will result in the abolished classes.

It can be readily accepted that the Qur'ān has unambiguously laid greatest emphasis on justice. It has categorically made it obligatory on Muslims to do justice in case an injustice has been done by someone to someone else. It has asked believers to rectify any injustice committed by anyone against anyone. It has repeatedly asked believers to undertake prompt delivery of justice. Apart from quick delivery of rectificatory or corrective justice, the believers are also exhorted to deliver commutative justice as immediately as possible. The Prophet has exhorted the believers to pay up the daily wages of the laborers before the sweats on his skin dries up. Numerous verses from the Qurān can be cited in which believers are asked to devise strategies leading to distributive justice. However, certain vital considerations in the very textual sources of Islām can be cited which mitigate against the very capability of man to deliver justice whether distributive, retributive or commutative. Take, for example, the problem of Free-Will and Determinism. This problem has radically challenged the monotheistic world-view. The monotheistic religions such as Judaism, Christianity and Islām underline beliefs in a God who is All-Pervading, Infinite, Transcendental, Universal and Eternal. He is the Lord, Master, Sustainer, Creator and Originator of the universe including man. He has guided mankind through the teachings of thousands of the prophets. On the Day of Judgment as and when He establishes it, He will be holding all human beings responsible for their actions, sending all righteous people to the blessings of paradise and all vicious people to terrors of hellfire. The monotheistic world-view especially its Islāmic version, deems man to be a rational subject as well as a free moral agent. However, along with the rational subjectivity and free moral agency of man, the Absolute Sovereignty of God is also underlined by the Qurān. Such a situation presents a textual paradox of the highest order: is man really free pitted as he is against an absolutely Sovereign God. While there are verses in the Qurān supporting moral responsibility of man, there are quantitatively far more numerous and qualitatively far more powerful verses in the Qurān which overwhelmingly establish the absolute Sovereignty of God. In the face of this paradox, Muslims philosophers advanced divergent perspective with regard to Divine supremacy and human responsibility.

There can be various shades of meaning with regard to the concept of justice. An analysis of justice can lead us to various forms of justice, viz. legal, social, political, ethical, Divine, distributive, reparative, retributive, etc. Western social, political and legal philosophy has been mainly concerned with retributive, reparative and distributive forms of justice. The main concern of the retributive theory of justice is to accord appropriate punishment to wrongdoers. The reparative theory of justice is mainly concerned with rectification of past wrongs. The distributive theory of justice has attracted social, political and legal thinkers across the entire globe. Both Western and Eastern social, political and legal philosophers have focused their attention on distributive justice. The distributive theory of justice is concerned with the faire distribution of social benefits and burdens among all the members of any given society.

Religions, across the globe, have always been profoundly concerned with those fundamental values which impart meaning and significance to human life. All religions, in their specific ways, have dealt with the question of justice and also advanced an explanation of injustice in social, political and economic domains of operation. Islam, through the Glorious Quran, has advanced a detailed conception of justice. It may be called Revelatory or Divine justice. Such a conception of justice is all-pervasive and capable of manifestation in all spheres of human operation. The Quran emphasizes on legal, theological, social, ethical as well as distributive, reparative and retributive forms of justice. The Quran features numerous verses on different aspects of justice. The Quranic verses with reference to theft, gambling, usury, adultery, the orphans, the needy, the poor, the workers, the women, the slaves etc, invariably refer to the establishment of justice and the elimination of injustice. In fact, we are exhorted to appropriate justice and eradicate injustice in all the domains of human operation. Most importantly, the Quranic verses lay greatest emphasis on distributive justice. We can clearly and categorically understand the overwhelming Quranic emphasis on distributive justice with reference to its verses on weaker sections of society, the institution of *Zakat*, alms giving, Prohibition, usury, law of inheritance etc. A faithful compliance to such verses of the Quran can hopefully prevent an accumulation of wealth in few of hands and also lead to welfare of disadvantaged sections of the society.

The Quran proclaims Allah to be the Sovereign authority over the entire universe. He is both the Ultimate Ruler and the Ultimate Legislator of the entire universe. The disclosure of or divulgement of God is made possible through revelation of the Divine Wisdom through the Quranic propositions to the Prophet Muhammad. The justice emanating from such Divine Wisdom may be designated as Divine justice or revelatory justice as against the natural or human or positive justice. Most of the Western social and political philosophers are having concern with natural justice rooted in the application of human reason. As against natural justice Divine justice is the product of Divine Wisdom as embodied in the scriptures such as Old Testament, New Testament, and the Quran etc.

It can be brought out that there is no necessary conflict or contradiction between Reason and Revelation. Propositions or revelations embodying justice can be appropriated only through reason. In view of the same, reason and revelation must essentially be in harmony with each other. In fact, philosophers and scholars within Islam have tried to reconcile Divine justice with natural justice. It was Aristotle who firstly talked of natural justice. His Muslim followers tried to reconcile the natural justice with Divine justice as embodied in the Qur'ān. Al-Kindī, Al-Fārābī, Ibn Sīnā, Ibn Rushd etc were some of the prominent followers of Aristotle who tried to harmonize natural justice with Divine justice. Such a tradition has continued down to modern times when Islamic thinkers and scholars are trying to reconcile natural justice as advanced by modern Western philosophers and Divine justice as embodied in the Qur'ānic revelations. Just as Ghazālī advanced a strident critique of Muslim Aristotelians, so contemporary Islamic revivalists are advancing critical appraisals of Islamic modernists. Muslim revivalists contend that the adoption of Western concept was not consistent with the Islamic tradition. Revivalists underline that any reconciliation between the Divine justice as embodied in the Qur'ān and natural justice as highlighted by modern Western philosophers, was simply impossible of attainment. Islamic modernists, on other hand, have been attempting such reconciliation. Revivalists, however, continue their opposition to such a reconciliation, bringing out that dependence on reason inevitably leads human beings beyond the limits set by revelation. Divine injunctions as outlined in the Qur'ān and their human interpretations can never be equated. The modern Islamic scholars do not question the authority of the revelation. They simply try to achieve an understanding of justice as advanced in Western philosophy and also make it intelligible to the followers of the Qur'ān. Such an understanding is possible without undermining the authority of the revelation. The fundamental assumption is that the justice arrived at by reason is one and the same as advanced by a recourse to revelation. The contemporary conflict between Islamic revivalists and Islamic modernists is born out of mutual suspicions. The revivalists are not necessarily against reason and Western philosophy. The modernists are not necessarily against revelation. However, revivalists do suspect that modernists want to underline the role of reason at the cost of revelation and modernists do suspect that revivalists do highlight the role of revelation at the cost of reason.

The Divine revelations on Prophet Muhammad were assembled in the Qurān comprising of thirty Chapters totaling up to more than six thousand verses. The Divine Wisdom was intimated to the people in the sayings and doings of Muhammad which together constitute the *Sunnah* and *Sīrah* of the Prophet. Thus, the Qurān and the *Sunnah* are the primary textual sources of Islām. All Islāmic beliefs, values, injunctions and teachings are developed out of the Qurān or Divine Revelations and the Divine Wisdom communicated to us through Muhammad. The concept of Divine Justice in Islām is also rooted in the Qurānic revelation and the Divine Wisdom advanced by the Prophet. For Muslims, the principles of justice as stipulated by the Qurān and the *Sunnah*, are infallible and inviolate. The Divine Justice as derived from the Qurān and *Sunnah* is considered by Muslims to be beyond space and time and universally and eternally applicable.

Theological justice is justice in accordance with the doctrines laid down by the theologians concerning God's attributes of Will and Essence. While the theologians were in agreement that theological justice, the *jus divinum* flows from God and that He is the final Judge, they disagreed on whether it is an expression of His Will and Power or an expression of His Essence and Perfection. The ramification of these differences proved so important that Muslim theologians were divided into two major schools, the school of Revelation and the school of Reason, each stressing one of the God's as overriding, resulting in a continuing debate on the nature of justice and on man's capacity to realize it on Earth as well as on the destiny of man in the hereafter.

Ethical justice is in accordance with the highest virtues which establish a standard of human conduct. In accordance with legal justice, man is commanded to observe a minimum standard of duties, but in accordance with ethical justice, man is commanded to conform to the highest possible standard of good. Justice, in the words of Aristotle, is "the greatest of virtues" and in it every virtue is comprehended. The highest virtues are taken to be implied in the Revelation, but Muslim writers have drawn their ethical standard not only from Islāmic but also from foreign (Greek, Persian and others) ethical sources. In their theories of ethical justice, they consciously sought to harmonize Islāmic justice with foreign notions and values. Like philosophical justice, ethical justice is discussed on two levels, Divine and human, and most writers tried to correlate the two, though some dealt with one or the other independently, making no effort to relate the one with other.

Legal justice is in accordance with the Law. Etymologically, justice is a legal term and the literal meaning of *jus* and *justum* necessarily overlap. However, the meaning of justice has been extended to imply not only legal but also other aspects. So law and justice may coincide, as some elements of justice may be embodied in the substance of law. In Islām, Law *(Sharī'ah)* is closely intertwined with Religion, and both are considered the expressions of God's Will and justice. The function of Religion is to define and determine goals, justice and others and the aim of Law is to indicate the path by virtue of which God's justice and other goals are realized.

Substantive justice is the internal aspect of law and the elements of justice contained in the law constitute a declaration of rights and wrong. In the Islāmic vocabulary the rights and wrongs are called the permissions and prohibitions *(al-halal wa al-haram)* and form the general and particular rules of the Islāmic law *(Sharī'ah)*. The Law does not specify under the categories of permission *(haram)* under the categories of permissions *(halal)* and prohibitions *(haram)*. What is the measure which distinguishes just from unjust acts, it merely states that believers must fulfill their duties *(farad)* under the first category and abstain from others under prohibitions. It was taken for granted that all obligatory acts must be just, as they are the expressions of God's Will and justice, and that all prohibited acts are unjust on the ground that the Revelation cannot inflict an injustice on believers. In their inquiry into the nature and scope of legal obligations, the scholars were able to discern the underlying principles governing the distinction between just and unjust acts. Taken together, these principles determine what the ultimate goals or purposes of the Law *(maqasid al- Sharī'ah)* ought to be.

CPSIA information can be obtained
at www.ICGtesting.com
Printed in the USA
LVHW021639120423
744200LV00009B/268